BLACK HOLES

AND OTHER
SPACE ODDITIES

BLACK
HOLES

AND OTHER
SPACE ODDITIES

By
Alex Barnett

Consultant
Stuart Clark

A DK Publishing Book

LONDON, NEW YORK, MUNICH,
MELBOURNE, and DELHI

Project Editor Matthew Turner
Project Art Editor Keith Davis
Senior Editor Fran Jones
Senior Art Editor Stefan Podhorodecki
Category Publisher Linda Martin
Managing Art Editor Jacquie Gulliver
US Editor Margaret Parrish
Picture Researcher Sarah Pownall
DK Picture Library Sarah Mills,
Rose Horridge
Production Jenny Jacoby
DTP Designer Siu Yin Ho

First American Edition, 2002

02 03 04 05 10 9 8 7 6 5 4 3 2 1

First published in the United States by
DK Publishing, Inc.
375 Hudson Street, New York, NY 10014

A Cataloging-in-Publication record for this title is
available from the Library of Congress

ISBN 0-7894-8844-2 (hc)
ISBN 0-7894-8845-0 (pb)

Reproduced by Colourscan, Singapore
Printed and bound by L.E.G.O., Italy

See our complete product line at
www.dk.com

CONTENTS

INTRODUCTION

Space is incredibly vast, and it's full
of surprises. There are worlds that
are hotter than the hottest furnace and
others that are colder than a freezer.
There are places that could poison you, roast
you, and drown you. There are galaxies that
"eat" each other, black holes that twist time
and space – and somewhere, on an unknown
planet, perhaps there are aliens looking at us.

This book will take you to all these places. It's your
launchpad to the Universe as well as your guide to
the exciting science of astronomy. You'll find out
about unusual features of the Sun, and the rocky and
gassy planets that make up our Solar System. You
can take a trip to the asteroid belt, which contains
much of the Solar System's
leftover junk – and
find out what
asteroids and
comets are
made of.

SPECTACULAR
EVENTS IN THE
SKY, SUCH AS
SOLAR ECLIPSES,
CAN BE SEEN
FROM
EARTH.

You'll also
learn about
the stars, and
how they are
born, live for
millions or
billions of
years, then
die. Some
blow up at the
end of their
lives, a few turn
into black holes –
crushed, dead stars
that lurk in space. This
book will even tell you
where they're hiding!

Space is truly exciting – and it's
hard to believe that it was born in a Big Bang more
than 10 billion years ago. Today, much of the
Universe still remains a mystery to scientists. The
great thing is, however, that we can see space with
our own eyes and journey in our minds to the farthest
galaxies and most distant worlds.

For those of you who want to explore this subject
in more detail, there are black "Log On" boxes that
appear throughout the book. These will direct you
to some fascinating websites, where you can find
out even more about
the mysteries of
the Universe.

So let's explore!

Alex Barnett

ENDLESS SPACE

The Universe is a word we use to describe the sum total of everything that exists – from Earth to the ends of outer space. Our planet may seem big to us, but like a grain of sand in a vast desert, it's just a tiny, tiny part of the Universe – which is so big that scientists can't measure it in miles or kilometers. We can easily become bewildered by the sheer size of it all, so let's start somewhere familiar – with the planet Earth!

Home planet

As our home, the planet Earth is a special place for us. But although the world seems big, it is in fact just the tiniest speck within the Universe. For a start, there are eight other planets traveling around the Sun, in oval paths known as orbits.

Some of the planets are orbited by smaller worlds known as moons. Astronomers (scientists who study space) call this collection of planets, moons, and the smaller chunks

THIS IMAGE SHOWS HOW A TOWN MIGHT APPEAR TO A SATELLITE LOOKING DOWN TO CHECK EARTH'S CLIMATE.

SEEN FROM SPACE, EARTH IS A BEAUTIFUL SIGHT, WITH ITS CONTINENTS AND OCEANS.

of rock and ice around them the Solar System. The Sun, which sits at the center of the Solar System, is a star.

Stars

A star is much bigger than a planet. It generates energy in its core and actually gives off light, but a

planet just reflects light. Like planets, there are many different types of stars. They differ in size, in the amount of matter they contain, and in the temperature of their surfaces. The Sun is an average yellow star.

The Galaxy

Like one house in a city, the Sun is just one star in several hundred billion that make up

THE SUN AND THE REST OF THE SOLAR SYSTEM SIT IN A SPIRAL ARM OF OUR GALAXY, ABOUT 30,000 LIGHT-YEARS FROM THE CENTER. STARS OF MANY TYPES CAN BE FOUND IN THE MILKY WAY.

THE SUN LOOKS HUGE, BUT IT'S ACTUALLY AN AVERAGE-SIZED STAR, ABOUT HALFWAY THROUGH ITS 9-BILLION-YEAR LIFE.

our Galaxy. Sometimes called the Milky Way, our Galaxy is composed of a flat, spiral pattern of stars around a central bulge of other stars. As well as stars and planets, the Milky Way contains vast gas clouds that will one day shrink to become new stars and planets.

Other galaxies

The Milky Way is, in turn, just one of billions of other galaxies. Some are also spiral-shaped, while others are just big, round collections of stars. The galaxies themselves tend to cluster together in both small and large groups. While a small group may contain 20 galaxies, in a large cluster there are thousands. These clusters of galaxies stretch across space like cobwebs

making a giant, cosmic spiderweb. Between the "cobwebs" are gigantic bubbles, called voids, in which hardly any galaxies or stars exist at all.

Light speed

Distances in space are so large that astronomers need a vast "space ruler" to measure them. So they use light-years. A light-year is the distance that light travels in one year.

You may not have realized that light moves – it seems to appear at the flick of a switch. In fact, it covers 190,000 miles (300,000 km) in a second! Imagine how many seconds there are in a year. That gives you an idea how far light can travel in a year. It's a long way!

M

EARTH

THESE PLANETS ARE NOT TO SCALE – IF THEY WERE, WE WOULDN'T GET THEM ALL ON THE PAGE. IN REALITY, YOU COULD FIT 11 EARTHS ACROSS JUPITER'S MIDDLE!

MERCURY

VENUS

PLUTO

NEPTUNE

URANUS

SATURN

JUPITER

URANUS, NEPTUNE, AND PLUTO
WERE NOT KNOWN TO THE
ANCIENT ASTRONOMERS.
THEY ARE VERY FAR AWAY.
LIGHT TAKES ABOUT FIVE
HOURS TO GET TO PLUTO!

Time-traveling When you look up at the stars in the night sky, you are actually looking back in time. The light you can see shining from distant stars started on its journey millions of years ago.

Think of it another way. Suppose you visited a friend this morning, and then you traveled for a few hours to see another friend. When the second friend asked you how the first friend was, you'd say "okay." But that was how your friend was a few hours ago, not how they are now.

Thinking about how light travels across the Solar System, we begin to see how big space is. For example, light travels from the Sun to Earth in about eight minutes, to Jupiter and Saturn in a couple of hours, and to Pluto in about five hours. But that light takes more than four years to reach the next star!

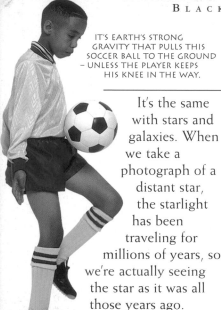

IT'S EARTH'S STRONG GRAVITY THAT PULLS THIS SOCCER BALL TO THE GROUND – UNLESS THE PLAYER KEEPS HIS KNEE IN THE WAY.

It's the same with stars and galaxies. When we take a photograph of a distant star, the starlight has been traveling for millions of years, so we're actually seeing the star as it was all those years ago. Weird, isn't it?

You have gravity, too. Just as you are pulled towars Earth, so Earth is pulled a tiny bit toward you. But because the Earth is so much more massive than you are, it doesn't notice!

E scaping gravity
Gravity doesn't go away once you get away from Earth, but it does weaken. If you travel fast enough, your high speed can counterbalance the pull of gravity back to Earth. When you are counterbalanced like this, you feel weightless, even though you're traveling at high speed. If you stop moving, or

MOST OF THE UNIVERSE IS NOTHING BUT EMPTY SPACE

M ay the force be with you
Physics tells us that light is the fastest thing in the Universe – nothing travels faster. But light speed isn't the only law of physics we have to observe when we explore the Universe. There's also gravity.

Gravity is a force that pulls things together. The more matter (mass) there is in one place, the stronger the pull. Earth is so big that it exerts its own gravitational force. That's why a soccer ball returns to the ground after you've kicked it.

slow down, then you will be pulled back to Earth. The Space Shuttle, for example, fires its thrusters in order to slow down and return to Earth.

U niversal force
The Sun's strong gravity keeps the planets in orbit around it. A much more powerful gravitational pull also keeps stars in orbit around the hub of the Galaxy. Gravity affects how

the stars are born, how they live, and how they die. It will also affect how the Universe finally ends.

THIS ASTRONAUT IS TRAVELING AT 17,000 MPH (27,000 KMH). HER HIGH SPEED STOPS GRAVITY FROM DRAGGING HER BACK TO EARTH.

telescopes in space, where the view is even clearer and they don't have to worry about daytime spoiling the view!

There are special telescopes that can pick up invisible radiation – radio waves, infrared, ultraviolet, X-rays, and gamma rays. All of this radiation carries information about the object it came from.

Astronomers also send probes – unmanned spacecraft – to explore the more distant objects in our Solar System.

As astronomers build bigger and more sensitive telescopes, and better computers with which to study the information, they understand more about the Universe. They don't understand it all yet!

Tools of the trade Astronomers make observations to test the laws of physics. They use many different tools to gather the information. You may have seen pictures of telescopes on mountaintops – put there to get above all the pollution on Earth. Astronomers also use

THE HUBBLE SPACE TELESCOPE PEERS INTO THE UNIVERSE. IT GATHERS INFORMATION ON OBJECTS WE CAN'T VISIT IN PERSON.

13

STAR STUFF

People have been wondering about stars for thousands of years, but it's only in the last couple of centuries that we have started to understand them. Stars may look like distant dots of light that never do anything, but nothing could be further from the truth. In fact, once you know more about stars, you'll probably be glad that they are so far away!

THE PLEIADES, OR SEVEN SISTERS, IS A CLUSTER OF YOUNG STARS, BORN "ONLY" ABOUT 60 MILLION YEARS AGO.

A star is born

If there were a universal recipe book, then the instructions for making a star would read something like this.
* Take a huge amount of gas, mostly hydrogen.
* Mix well with a little other stuff, like carbon and oxygen.
* Allow gravity to squish the mixture together into a large, spinning ball.
* Squeeze the spinning ball until its center reaches about 18 million °F (10 million °C) and nuclear reactions start. Now you have a star.

It sounds simple enough, but if you were the celestial cook, you'd have to wait a very long time to see the end result. It can take millions of years for a star to be born!

The ingredients for stars exist all over the Universe. In our own Galaxy we see big clouds of gas and dust. But for stars to start forming, something needs to stir up the cloud so that bits of it start clumping together. The "stirrer" might be a shock

THE ORION NEBULA IS A SWIRLING CLOUD OF GAS AND DUST FROM WHICH STARS ARE BEING BORN. THE STARS LIGHTING UP THE GAS ARE JUST A FEW MILLION YEARS OLD.

WEIRD WORLD
IF A BALL OF GAS FORMS THAT IS
LESS THAN ONE-TENTH THE SIZE
OF THE SUN, THEN IT WILL
NEVER BECOME A STAR. WE
CALL SUCH A BALL A BROWN
DWARF. THE PLANET JUPITER
IS ALMOST BIG ENOUGH TO
BE A FAILED STAR.

wave from a nearby star exploding. If so, then gravity takes over and each clump attracts more gas and dust, which attracts more, and so on. The more star stuff you gather together, the stronger gravity pulls. This squeezes the gas, making it hotter. Eventually it gets so hot that nuclear reactions start in the middle.

Striking a balance
If you're that star, then the moment those nuclear reactions kick in, you've won your first battle against gravity. The energy flowing outward and making you "shine" balances the pull of gravity inward. Stars need to use up millions of tons of mass each second in nuclear reactions just to keep gravity from winning the battle.

A star's birth is dramatic. Once the star "switches on," then it blows away much the cloud of gas and dust from which it was born, and from which any orbiting planets will already have been formed.

Nuclear notes
What's really happening in the middle of a star? If you had a telescope powerful enough, you'd notice that in the middle of the star, all the hydrogen atoms are whizzing around. When the atoms collide with each other, they fuse (stick together). It takes four hydrogen atoms to fuse in order to make helium. When that happens, some energy is produced. This is called nuclear fusion and it's how stars shine.

Big and small
Stars aren't all the same size. Some are several times smaller than the Sun, while other stars

THE HUBBLE SPACE TELESCOPE TOOK THIS AWESOME PICTURE OF STARS BEING BORN. THE TOWERING CLOUDS CONTAIN THE GAS AND DUST FROM WHICH THEY ARE MADE.

are 20 or 30 times larger! If you want to know what will happen to a star during its life, and how it will die, then the only thing you need to know is how big it is.

Massive stars have bigger problems with gravity. Remember that the more mass you have, the stronger the pull of gravity. Therefore, a big star has to use up fuel much more rapidly to keep winning the battle against gravity. That means that it won't last as long as a small star. A big star might last for 50 million years, but

a small star could easily last for 5 billion years. Being big is not always a good thing!

Clues in colors

Stars are also different colors. You might not have spotted it, but next time it's a clear night, have a good look at the stars. Some are whiter than others. Some appear reddish or orange.

You can tell how hot a star is by looking at its color. If you think about putting an

WEIRD WORLD

FIGHTING GRAVITY IS EXTREMELY HARD WORK! EVERY SECOND, OUR SUN PRODUCES AS MUCH ENERGY AS 4 TRILLION TRILLION 100-WATT LIGHT-BULBS.

iron poker into a fire, as it heats up it begins to glow a dull red. As it gets hotter, it goes yellow and then white. At its hottest, it glows a blue-white and is painful to look at. So the coolest stars are red

BETELGEUSE IS A RED GIANT, A STAR CLOSE TO THE END OF ITS LIFE. THIS IS HOW IT MAY LOOK WHEN IT FINALLY EXPLODES.

That's hot. The fact that blue stars are the hottest might seem odd if you are used to having red mark the hot water and

MOST STARS IN OUR GALAXY ARE THE SUN'S SIZE OR SMALLER

stars. Some have a surface temperature of just a few thousand degrees. The hottest stars are blue-white and can have a surface temperature of perhaps 90,000 °F (50,000 °C).

blue mark the cold water. Just remember that in the Universe, the colors are reversed!

Generally, the hottest stars are also the largest. Since they have to burn fuel very rapidly to overcome gravity, they shine much more brightly than the smaller stars and can be seen at a greater distance.

Starlight, star bright

How can we find out about the stars if they are so far away? In the last century, a philosopher (thinker) once said that we could never know what the stars were made of. Luckily for us he was wrong. The light from a star is like a fingerprint, and it can tell us all we need to know about it.

Astronomers capture the light from a star and split it up using an instrument called a spectroscope. By studying the light they can tell what the star is made of, how hot it is, how it is moving, and plenty of other useful data.

When you think about it, it's amazing how the twinkling light from stars means we actually don't have to wonder what they are – we know!

Doubling up

Usually many stars are born from the same cloud of gas and dust. Sometimes stars are born so close together that their gravity holds them together for the rest of their lives.

DOUBLE STARS, LOCKED TOGETHER BY GRAVITY, SPEND THEIR ENTIRE LIVES ORBITING ONE ANOTHER.

LOG ON...
http://starchild.
gsfc.nasa.gov

Just as our Sun has planets orbiting it, so some stars orbit each other. It turns out that nearly half the stars in our galaxy have companions, and in some cases they have more than one.

Death of a star

Eventually, all stars run out of fuel – and that's when it gets really interesting.

A small star, such as our Sun, burns its fuel slowly and steadily, turning hydrogen into helium. Eventually it runs out of hydrogen in its center. At that point, gravity takes over and starts to squeeze the helium. The center of the star gets hotter and hotter.

The star swells up into a huge red giant star, and it becomes unstable. At the end of its life, the star's outer layers puff off

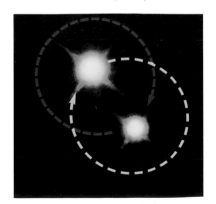

Weird World

The Crab Nebula is the remnant of a dead star 6,000 light-years away from Earth. According to Chinese history books, the star exploded in a flash on July 4, 1054.

into space, forming a cosmic smoke ring. This is called a planetary nebula.

The dead core of the star that remains slowly cools, but it's a very weird dead star called a white dwarf. Gravity is squeezing it so much that just a spoonful of white dwarf stuff would weigh as much as an elephant!

S upernovas

For the bigger stars, when gravity starts to squeeze the helium it can get hot enough for nuclear reactions to start again. Large stars burn helium into products such as carbon and oxygen. However, each source of fuel only lasts a very

scattering itself through space. A star in these explosive death throes is known as a supernova.

B right beacons

Just a few stars each year end their lives with a bang. When we look into the skies, we see these exploding stars in other galaxies, and they briefly outshine their whole galaxy. The energy that a supernova gives out in a few seconds is about equal to the Sun's output over 9 billion years!

S tardust

When a really big star explodes, the temperature can reach more than 90 billion °F (50 billion °C). In that instant,

OUR BODIES ARE MADE FROM THE DUST OF DEAD, EXPLODED STARS

short while before the squeezing and burning cycle has to start all over again.

Eventually the star ends up with a core made of iron. Iron can't be used as a nuclear fuel: fusing iron takes in energy instead of giving it out. The energy source switches off and gravity wins. The star explodes,

all the other elements – including gold, uranium, lead, and so on – are created. This stardust is spread throughout the Universe, joining clouds of gas and dust. These then form other stars.

Around some of those stars, planets are created – and in our case at least, those elements went on to form life. It may sound really corny, but it's true. We're all made of stardust!

THE BRIGHT RINGS OF THIS PLANETARY NEBULA ARE THE PUFFED-OFF REMAINS OF THE HOT, DYING STAR AT THE CENTER.

BLACK HOLES

Y ou're a big star. You've burned fast and bright, then exploded in a supernova. After a blinding flash, most of you has scattered across space, but your core remains and there's a lot of it. The enormous pull of your gravity is impossible to resist. You're set to become one of the weirdest objects that we know of … a black hole!

AT THE DARK HEART OF A SPINNING WHORL OF SPACE MATTER IS A BLACK HOLE. THE AWESOME GRAVITY OF A DEAD STAR SUCKS EVERYTHING INTO THE MIDDLE – EVEN OTHER STARS!

Gravity wins

Black holes seem almost in the realms of science fiction. We know a few things about them, and they give us some interesting ideas about other universes and time travel. But black holes aren't really that complicated.

Remember that the more massive a star is, the stronger the force of gravity. It was okay for the star to be big when it had lots of energy from nuclear reactions flowing outward to balance the pull of gravity. But as soon as those reactions stop, gravity takes over.

WEIRD WORLD

AS THE FORCE OF GRAVITY OVERPOWERS IT AND FORCES IT TO COLLAPSE, A DYING STAR CAN BE SQUEEZED BY A HUGE AMOUNT. A STAR SEVERAL TIMES THE SIZE OF THE SUN BECOMES A BLACK HOLE THE SIZE OF A SMALL TOWN.

two negatively charged particles to get too close together. For small dead stars, this "pushing away" force in their core is enough to prevent the star from collapsing completely.

Bigger stars have strong enough gravity to force the positive and negatively charged particles to squish together. When they do this, they become neutrons – particles with no charge. And when the neutrons are packed "shoulder to shoulder" in the dead star, then the star stops collapsing.

HOT GASES THAT SWIRL AROUND BIG BLACK HOLES RELEASE X-RAYS

Fighting back

We know of a couple of ways to fight back against gravity. The star stuff left in a dead star is made up of positively or negatively charged particles. Just as two magnets with the same polarity push each other away, it's difficult to force

But for really big dead stars that have more matter than three times the size of the Sun, there is nothing that can balance gravity. The star collapses, and keeps on collapsing.

Warping space and time

So where do the "black" and "hole" bits come in? It's often easier to think of gravity in a different way.

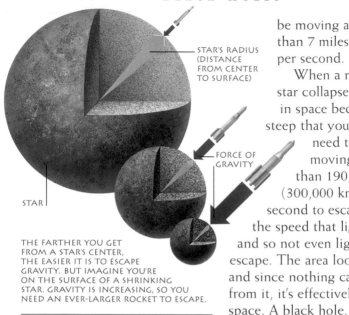

STAR'S RADIUS
(DISTANCE
FROM CENTER
TO SURFACE)

FORCE OF
GRAVITY

STAR

THE FARTHER YOU GET
FROM A STAR'S CENTER,
THE EASIER IT IS TO ESCAPE
GRAVITY. BUT IMAGINE YOU'RE
ON THE SURFACE OF A SHRINKING
STAR. GRAVITY IS INCREASING, SO YOU
NEED AN EVER-LARGER ROCKET TO ESCAPE.

be moving at more than 7 miles (11 km) per second.

When a really big star collapses, the bend in space becomes so steep that you would need to be moving at more than 190,000 miles (300,000 km) per second to escape. That's the speed that light travels, and so not even light can escape. The area looks "black," and since nothing can escape from it, it's effectively a hole in space. A black hole.

Hunting the invisible
If they are black, how do we know they exist? More importantly, how can we find one? Well, if we can't see the black hole directly, perhaps we can see how it affects something else.

Dark companions
Since many stars have companions, then it's possible that a sunlike star might have a companion that is a really giant star. The giant star will zip through its life, ending with a bang and becoming a black hole. The sunlike star

Imagine you have a rubber sheet, and you place a ball in the middle of the sheet. It will make the sheet bend. Anything that passes too close to where the sheet bends will roll in toward the ball.

That ball is like a star, and the rubber sheet shows what gravity is doing to space – it bends it. If you wanted to get away from the ball, you'd have to have enough energy to get out of the dip in the sheet. Planet Earth causes a bend in space, and to escape the gravity of Earth, you have to

WEIRD WORLD
BLACK HOLES GROW AS THEY SWALLOW STUFF. SOME OF THE BIGGEST MAY HAVE ACTUALLY SWALLOWED OTHER BLACK HOLES.

LOG ON... http://amazing-space.stsci.edu/blackholes/

will still be shining. But when that sunlike star evolves to become a red giant star, then its outer layers will get closer to the black hole, and the black hole will start to steal away the gas.

The gas will form a swirling disc, called an accretion disc, around the black hole. It's a bit like the way water swirls around the drain before it goes down.

Looking for clues

The accretion disc gets heated up to several million degrees as it swirls around. Gas this hot doesn't just glow – it gives off X-rays! In 1970, a satellite called *Uhuru* detected X-rays coming from an area next to an

enormous blue giant star. When astronomers took a look, they worked out that an object that the blue star was orbiting was about 10 times larger than the Sun. However, the object didn't shine. It was the first black hole to be discovered, and it is called Cygnus X-1.

Central monsters

If you're impressed by a black hole made from several times the amount of stuff as the Sun,

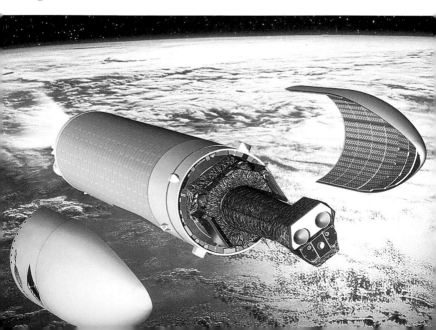

XMM-NEWTON, A HUGE TELESCOPE, IS PUT INTO SPACE. NEWTON LOOKS FOR X-RAYS, TELLTALE SIGNS OF DISTANT BLACK HOLES.

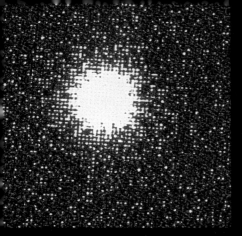

THIS IMAGE, TAKEN IN SPACE BY AN X-RAY TELESCOPE, SHOWS X-RAY ENERGY STREAMING AWAY FROM A BLACK HOLE.

and they seem to coincide with an age where strange objects called quasars were around. Quasars are some of the most distant objects we can see. They are incredibly bright, which suggests that they are being powered by great energy.

Close to home

Here's the troubling part. There seems to be a black hole at the center of our own Galaxy. X-ray and radio telescopes have picked up powerful sources at the galactic center. They show very hot gas swirling around something massive in the middle and smaller jets of materials being blasted out. Although it isn't as active as some black holes we see in other galaxies, you still wouldn't want to get too close!

you should see the monsters that appear to be at the center of most galaxies. Some of them contain as much star stuff as millions of Suns! Black holes that big can only be trouble, and when we look at galaxies in the Universe, we see some violent things going on.

In some galaxies, huge jets of stuff are blasted out from the centers. These are made up of matter thrown off a giant disc

THE BIGGEST KNOWN BLACK HOLE WEIGHS ABOUT 100 MILLION SUNS

of gas and ripped-up stars which is swirling really fast around the big black hole.

These super-massive black holes were probably formed very early on in the Universe,

The waiting game

Once a black hole has pulled in any gas and dust that is lying around nearby, it will lurk silently waiting for more matter to come its way.

Stranger than fiction
Hollywood films like *Time Bandits* and *Stargate* use black holes as a convenient way to travel in time and space. The reason they can come up with such unlikely sounding stories is because astronomers have predicted that black holes can have some very strange properties.

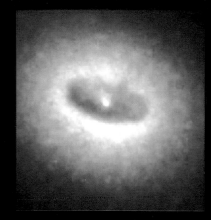

SCIENTISTS FIGURE THAT BLACK HOLES LIE AT THE CENTERS OF GALAXIES. THIS IS A CLOUD OF GAS, DUST, AND STARS MASSED AROUND A BLACK HOLE.

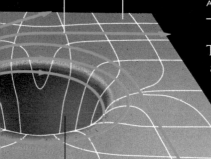

RAYS OF LIGHT   SPACE

GRAVITY WELL OF BLACK HOLE

THIS DIAGRAM SHOWS A BLACK HOLE'S GRAVITY AS A DEEP "WELL" IN SPACE.

THE BLUE LINES ARE LIGHT WAVES, MOVING AT 190,000 MPH (300,000 KMH).

SOME WAVES ARE MERELY BENT AS THEY PASS NEAR THE WELL. THOSE THAT STRAY OVER THE EVENT HORIZON – THE POINT OF NO RETURN – ARE SUCKED IN FOREVER.

LIGHT SUCKED INTO GRAVITY WELL

The true edge of a black hole is a place from which, once you pass it, there is no turning back. You will no longer be able to escape the gravity of the black hole. And the trouble is, we don't know what happens next. Because no information about what's beyond this point can reach us, we have no way of knowing about any events that happen beyond this point. For that reason, it's known as the event horizon.

Singularly dense
In the middle of a black hole, we expect to find a region where the entire dead star has been squashed to a single

27

point. This point is called the singularity. Anything falling past the event horizon are squashed out of existence at the singularity.

Some astronomers believe that black holes will be rotating, in which case the singularity will actually be a ring. This means that we might be able to pass through it.

The big squeeze

You may be a brave black-hole traveler, but you still want to be choosy about the type of hole you decide to fall into.

If you picked a hole that was created by a dead star – as opposed to a big black hole at the center of a galaxy – then you would certainly kill yourself. This type of black hole bends space very steeply, so your feet would be pulled far more than your head. You would be stretched longer and thinner and "spaghettified"!

Black holes such as those in the middle of galaxies, which are several million times the mass of the Sun, bend space in a more gentle way. So assuming you had already survived the raging storm of X-rays and other violent happenings near the black hole, you just might survive a trip through the black hole itself.

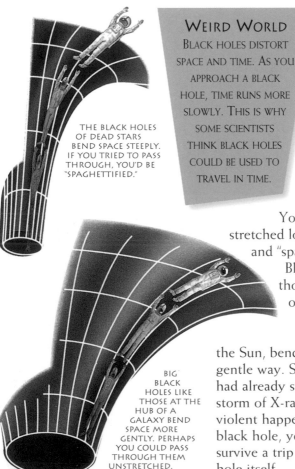

THE BLACK HOLES OF DEAD STARS BEND SPACE STEEPLY. IF YOU TRIED TO PASS THROUGH, YOU'D BE "SPAGHETTIFIED."

BIG BLACK HOLES LIKE THOSE AT THE HUB OF A GALAXY BEND SPACE MORE GENTLY. PERHAPS YOU COULD PASS THROUGH THEM UNSTRETCHED.

WEIRD WORLD
BLACK HOLES DISTORT SPACE AND TIME. AS YOU APPROACH A BLACK HOLE, TIME RUNS MORE SLOWLY. THIS IS WHY SOME SCIENTISTS THINK BLACK HOLES COULD BE USED TO TRAVEL IN TIME.

A BLACK HOLE MIGHT BE A BRIDGE, OR WORMHOLE, THAT ENABLES US TO TRAVEL BETWEEN OUR UNIVERSE AND ANOTHER.

EXIT INTO ANOTHER UNIVERSE

Space travel

What might you find if you were able to travel through a black hole? Some scientists think that if you passed through a rotating circular singularity, then you would come out into another universe. This is called an Einstein-Rosen bridge, after the two scientists who thought it up.

The problem is that any information can't pass back over the event horizon, so if you did offer to go through a black hole, and you found a wonderful universe on the other side, you couldn't come back and tell anyone about it.

Wormholes

Kip Thorne, an American scientist, believes that it might be possible to create these bridges, called wormholes, in our own Galaxy. This would enable people to travel between the stars almost instantly.

The problem is, apart from the fact that we aren't quite sure how to create the wormhole in the first place, it looks like we'd need to invent some sort of antigravity material to keep the wormhole in place once we'd set it up! This is because scientists know that such a hole would only last for a very short time before collapsing. Only something that could oppose the force of gravity would be able to keep the hole open.

TIME TRAVEL COMES TRUE IN FILMS SUCH AS BACK TO THE FUTURE. COULD WE USE BLACK HOLES TO JOURNEY TO THE PAST?

29

OUR CLOSEST STAR

The Sun, our closest star, is a vast ball
of burning, seething gases that has
sat at the hub of our Solar System for more
than 5 billion years. The Sun gives off all
kinds of radiation. Some provides heat and light,
which keeps our Earth at the right temperature.
Other radiation
from the Sun
is deadly.

THIS IS A CROSS-
SECTION OF THE
SUN. NUCLEAR
REACTIONS AT
THE CORE SEND
ENERGY (LIGHT
AND OTHER
RADIATION)
INTO SPACE.

ENERGY FLOWS OUT
THROUGH THE
CONVECTIVE ZONE

PHOTOSPHER
(SUN'S SURFAC

CORONA
(HALO O
GASES)

CONVECTIVE ZONE

CORE

C lose up
We can't go
to the Sun – it's
dangerous even to
look at it! But scientists
now have a fair idea of what it's
like at close range, from its
core to its outer atmosphere.

Deep in the Sun's core, a
continous nuclear reaction is
taking place. Hydrogen atoms
are forced together in the heat
and turn into helium. Energy
created by this reaction makes
its way to the Sun's surface and
into space, reaching us as light
and other radiation.

The visible
surface of the
Sun is called the
photosphere, which means
"sphere of light." The sunlight
that we're familiar with comes
from this surface. At about
9,900 °F (5,500 °C) the surface
is very hot, but it's nothing
compared to the center of the
Sun, which is almost 3,000
times hotter. Phew!

IN AN IMAGE OF THE SUN TAKEN IN
ULTRAVIOLET LIGHT, ACTIVE AREAS ON
THE SURFACE APPEAR WHIT

WEIRD WORLD
SUNSPOTS ARE DARK BECAUSE
THEY'RE COOLER THAN THE GAS
AROUND THEM. BY WATCHING
THEM MOVE, ASTRONOMERS
KNOW THAT THE SUN'S
EQUATOR SPINS FASTER
THAN ITS POLES.

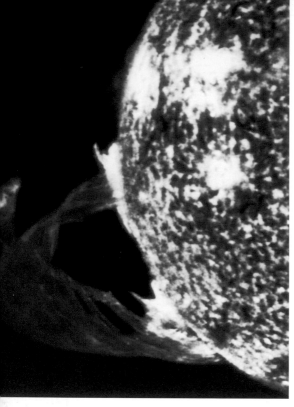

around the Sun during a total solar eclipse. The corona is made up of gas heated to more than 1.8 million °F (1 million °C). Scientists believe this is heated by changes in the Sun's magnetic field.

Wind from the Sun

The corona is the source of the "solar wind." This is a stream of charged particles that flows out from the Sun at a speed of more than 250 miles (400 km) per second. That's fast! The solar wind flows in all directions and stretches a long way. Spacecraft venturing beyond the orbit of Pluto, our most distant planet, can still detect the solar wind.

Storms from space

The solar wind is gusty and can affect the planets. These gusts are caused by huge eruptions, or flares, on the Sun's surface. Sometimes, when the eruptions blow matter off the surface, they can be dangerous.

Dark spots, flares, and other features mark the surface of the Sun. The spots are caused by magnetism. The Sun has a north and south magnetic pole, like Earth, and the magnetic field disturbs the hot, gassy surface, creating the spots. Sunspots can be huge, up to four times the size of Earth! Most last for a few weeks or months before they disappear.

Like Earth, the Sun has an atmosphere. This atmosphere, called the corona ("crown"), extends far into space. You can see it as a halo of white light

Solar storms damage satellites and also endanger astronauts, who don't have Earth's air to protect them from the harmful radiation. To protect the astronauts, experts regularly check the solar weather, and space walks or satellite launches are delayed if there are warnings that a solar storm is brewing.

Earth in danger

Earth's atmosphere and magnetic field protect us from some, but not all, of this solar radiation. Strong storms can give airplane passengers the equivalent dose of several chest X-rays and knock out power supplies, plunging entire cities into darkness.

When a solar storm is giving Earth a beating, it excites the air at the top of our atmosphere and makes it glow. These amazing glows are often called the northern lights, but they can also happen around the South Pole (southern lights).

The good news is that our Sun is not too close – in fact, it's an average 94 million miles (150 million km) away.

Finding out more

Because it affects our lives in so many ways, scientists are eager to discover more about the Sun. For instance, they know it doesn't only produce visible light. It gives off radio waves, X-rays, infrared and ultraviolet rays. By taking pictures with cameras that pick up these other rays, scientists can learn a lot about the Sun's activities.

Many of these cameras are mounted on spacecraft and can photograph places where no human can go. For example, scientists can't see the Sun's poles (top and bottom) from Earth. In order to study these parts, they send out probes. A probe named *Ulysses* has been circling the Sun's poles since 1990.

One of the best space weather reporters is SOHO (short for SOlar Heliospheric Observatory). SOHO leads a lonely life out in space between

THESE EERIE GLOWS IN THE SKY ARE THE NORTHERN LIGHTS, SOMETIMES CALLED THE AURORA BOREALIS.

LOOKING DIRECTLY AT THE SUN CAN BLIND YOU – DON'T TRY IT!

Earth and the Sun. It picks up passing solar weather and warns experts of danger. It also sends back great pictures of surface eruptions – even of comets falling into the Sun.

Making the Solar System

We've learned that when a star is born, it is surrounded by a disc of gas and dust. So it was with our Sun, a long time ago. Some of the gas and dust stuck together and, over millions of years, formed our Solar System – the collection of planets and other rocks that orbit the Sun.

Searching other suns

Ours is not the only solar system in space. Astronomers believe planets are forming around many young stars. They call these planets "extrasolar planets." Some are large, even bigger than Jupiter, but the

WEIRD WORLD
ENERGY MAKES A ZIGZAG
COURSE FROM THE SUN'S
CORE AND TAKES 300,000
YEARS TO REACH ITS
SURFACE. FROM THERE,
IT ZIPS TO EARTH IN
JUST EIGHT MINUTES!

search is on for smaller, more Earthlike planets that might support life.

E nd of an era

What's the point in looking for other planets like Earth? Well, the Sun won't shine forever. Eventually, it will run out of hydrogen fuel and die. Toward the end of its life, the Sun will swell up and destroy Mercury, Venus, and Earth. Mars will also become rather hot, but will probably survive.

So if we Earthlings want to avoid a toasting, first we'll need to escape to a new world. But don't start packing yet, since the end isn't expected for another 5 billion years or so!

BEFORE IT DIES, THE SUN WILL SWELL INTO A RED GIANT STAR AND BAKE OUR PLANET TO A CINDER, BEFORE ENGULFING IT.

ROCKY PLANETS

Leftovers are often the best part – and the leftovers from the birth of our Sun are really fascinating. They include nine planets, as well as many smaller chunks of rock and ice. The four planets circling closest to the Sun are known as the rocky planets. They are Mercury, Venus, Earth, and Mars – and although they might be made of rock, that's about all they have in common.

Scarred Mercury

Way back when the planets were formed, the Solar System was a much more violent place than it is now. For millions of years, smaller bits of rock crashed into the planets, causing huge craters and cracks.

Mercury, the closest planet to the Sun, has no wind, rain, or volcanoes to cover up the evidence of being battered. So when we look at Mercury, we see the most cratered of all the planets.

Not that you'd want to visit Mercury for a closer look at its craters. By day, its surface is heated to 724 °F (420 °C) – enough to melt lead. By night, it plummets to nearly –392 °F (–200 °C)

because there is almost no atmosphere to act as a blanket and keep the planet warm.

So far, scientists have sent just one probe to Mercury, and it took pictures of only one area. They hope to send another spacecraft, named *Bepi-Colombo*, to find out more about this extraordinary "oven and freezer" world.

clouds. It's only in the last few decades that experts have developed instruments powerful enough to peer through the clouds.

MANY OF MERCURY'S FEATURES ARE NAMED AFTER FAMOUS COMPOSERS

Unlovely Venus

Though Venus is named after the Roman goddess of love, this planet is as far from lovely as you can get. It's covered in extremely thick, yellowish

Since Venus is almost the same size as Earth, some scientists had thought Venus might be a slightly warmer, wetter version of our planet – perhaps with jungles and oceans! But they now know that Venus is more like a

AT FIRST SIGHT, MERCURY'S PITTED AND SCARRED SURFACE LOOKS RATHER LIKE THE MOON.

house of horrors. It took
several attempts to land
a spacecraft on the
planet's surface, where
the blanket of gases is
so thick and heavy that
it crushes probes in an
instant. Just think what
it would do to you!

All the gases act like a
greenhouse, holding in
the Sun's heat. They
keep Venus baking hot –
even hotter than Mercury.
It's worth remembering that
if we don't take more care
with Earth's atmosphere, we
could end up overheating, too.

Acid rain

A trip to Venus
would be no
picnic either.
For a start, you
wouldn't be able
to see the Sun or
stars through the
clouds. Worse still,
this stormy planet crackles and
bangs ceaselessly with lightning
and thunder, and its rain is
made of sulfuric acid that
would reduce you to a crisp!
There's one small mercy,
though – Venus is so hot that
the rain boils away before it
reaches the ground.

WEIRD WORLD
VENUS ROTATES JUST ONCE
EVERY 243 DAYS. THAT'S
LONGER THAN THE 225
DAYS IT TAKES TO GO
AROUND THE SUN.

Life on Earth

The third rock
from the Sun is
Earth, and it has a very special
atmosphere – the thin layer
of air that surrounds our planet.
The air acts like a blanket. It
keeps Earth at exactly the right
temperature, allowing water to
exist in liquid form. Water is a
basic requirement for animal
and plant life.

Unlike the other planets, Earth has lots of oxygen in its atmosphere, enabling us to breathe. It wasn't always that way. Once there was more carbon dioxide, but when life began billions of years ago, it altered the balance. The atmosphere continues to change, and it is so essential to life that scientists use satellites to monitor it constantly.

S oft on the inside
Our Earth is changing all the time. Beneath the crust, the rock is still molten, like lava, and the solid plates of crust

THERE ARE ACTIVE VOLCANOES ON VENUS. IN THIS IMAGE MADE BY RADAR, THE HOTTEST ROCK IS YELLOW.

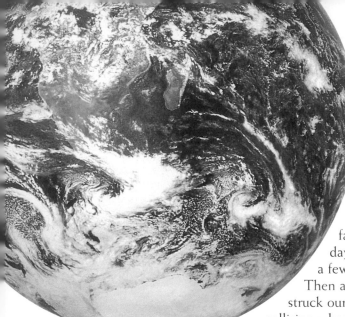

Many experts think that when Earth was new, it didn't have a Moon. It spun fast, too, with a day that was only a few hours long! Then a huge rock struck our planet. The collision whacked a lot of rock into space, where it settled in a ring around Earth. Over time, the rocky bits formed a clump and became the Moon.

float on the "runny rock." Over time, these plates collide and grind together. They make mountains, form volcanoes, and squeeze rock back down to the runny innards. This "recycling" of Earth's surface explains why we see fewer impact craters than on Mercury.

Mother Moon

When the Moon came into being, its gravity pulled on Earth and created the tides. These tides made it difficult for

THE PULL OF THE MOON'S GRAVIT ON OUR OCEANS CREATES TIDES

Chip off the old block

Like many of the planets, Earth is orbited by a moon. Normally, moons are much smaller than their "parent" planets. But our Moon is only four times smaller than Earth.

Earth to turn. Longer days could have helped life get started. The tides might have helped the first sea life move out onto land. Who knows – without our big Moon, maybe we wouldn't be here!

High and dry

The Moon itself is lifeless, with no air or liquid water. With no air, there is no wind, so the footprints the Moon-walkers made will never blow away. The American flag they set up in July 1969 stood out stiffly – but only with the help of a piece of wire!

Space probes have recently found ice at the Moon's south pole, at the bottom of craters where no Sun shines. Water is essential if we want to spend a long time on the Moon, building a base from which we can mine metals and minerals and explore space further.

Mars, the red planet

If astronauts explore another planet, they'll probably start with Mars – one of the most interesting of all the planets.

Mars is smaller than Earth, and its year is twice as long – although its day is only about half an hour longer. Mars has seasons, but they, too, are each twice as long. A long summer sounds great – or does it? On a summer's day on Mars you'd be lucky if the temperature rose to freezing point. You can't even imagine the winter!

THE MOON'S WINDLESS SURFACE IS POCKMARKED WITH COUNTLESS IMPACT CRATERS CAUSED BY METEORITES.

THICK CLOUDS OF RED DUST, WHIPPED UP BY POWERFUL SURFACE WINDS, GIVE MARS ITS PALE PINK HAZE.

Surface of Mars

Mars has a thin atmosphere, and what there is we couldn't breathe. Astronauts would need their own oxygen supply. But there's lots of oxygen locked in the iron-rich, rusty-red rocks.

Mars has the largest canyon in the Solar System. Mariner

WEIRD WORLD
IN 1877 AN ITALIAN, GIOVANNI SCHIAPARELLI, SAW LINES ON MARS AND CALLED THEM CANALI, OR "CHANNELS." ENGLISH SPEAKERS THOUGHT HE MEANT CANALS – MADE BY MARTIANS!

Valley is so big that it would stretch all the way across the US from New York to San Francisco.

Mars also has the mightiest volcanoes. Its largest, called Olympus Mons, is several times higher than Mount Everest. Luckily, it's extinct!

IN SOME PLACES MARINER VALLEY ON MARS IS OVER 47 MILES (75 KM) WIDE AND NEARLY 4 MILES (7 KM) DEEP.

Earth-like Mars?

With its polar caps, valleys, and mountains, Mars looks almost like Earth, except for the lack of water. Scientists think that long ago, water did flow on Mars, but a gradual thinning of its atmosphere, caused by solar radiation, led to the planet cooling down. As a result, the water probably froze deep below ground.

Over the next few years, a number of space probes are traveling toward Mars to seek out the water. They will also look for evidence that when Mars was warmer and wetter, some kind of life existed.

LOG ON...
www.seds.org/
nineplanets/nineplanets

Potatoes

Long ago, two small pieces of rock came close enough to Mars to be trapped by its gravity. They became the two moons and look rather like potatoes. They are called Phobos, meaning "fear," and Deimos, meaning "terror." Good names for the

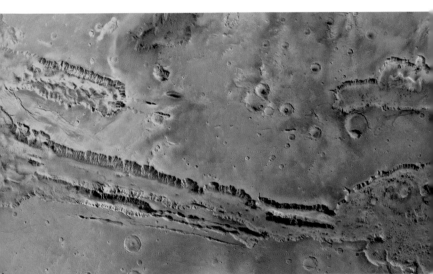

moons of the planet named after the god of war! These moons are tiny, with feeble gravity. If you were on Phobos and stepped off a 3.3-ft (1-m) ledge, it would take you about an hour to land on the surface.

Phobos is being pulled very slowly toward Mars, so that in perhaps a billion years, it will crash into the surface.

PHOBOS AND DEIMOS LOOK LIKE SOME OF THE ASTEROIDS. EVEN THOUGH THEY ARE SMALL, THEY ARE STILL HEAVILY CRATERED.

43

GASSY PLANETS

Beyond the rocky planets lie the gas giants – Jupiter, Saturn, Uranus, and Neptune. Far from the Sun, they are bitterly cold and dark. The cold has helped the planets build up thick coats of gas, which could not have formed if they were closer to the Sun. Beneath all that gas, the planets probably have rocky cores. Beyond the gas giants, there is one final planet – tiny, icy Pluto, the last stop in our Solar System.

Distant worlds

The outer planets are very, very remote. If you gazed back at the Sun from, say, the surface of Uranus, it wouldn't look like the Sun at all, but like a very bright star.

It takes many years for space probes to travel the vast distances from Earth, so it's hardly surprising that the outer planets are still largely unexplored mysteries.

Giant Jupiter

On a trip outward from the Sun, the first gas planet we would come to is Jupiter. Jupiter is the largest of the planets in our Solar System – it would be about

two-and-a-half times bigger than a ball made up of all the other planets combined!

Spots and bands

Despite its enormous size, Jupiter spins rapidly, making a complete rotation in less than 10 hours. This high rate of spin causes the gas to bulge out around the equator.

Jupiter is famous for its reddish, orange, and white clouds. They make up bands around the planet, so that it looks like a giant hard candy.

Where the different bands meet, storms and hurricanes rage. The most famous hurricane is known as the Great Red Spot. It has been blowing for more than three centuries and is large enough to swallow a couple of Earths!

JUPITER IS BANDED WITH SWIRLING CLOUDS. EXACTLY WHAT MAKES THEM SO COLORFUL IS STILL A MYSTERY.

Mighty moons

Jupiter has four large moons, spotted by Italian astronomer Galileo Galilei in the 1600s.

Io, the nearest of these moons, is squeezed and pulled hard by Jupiter's gravity. This causes tides, heating Io so much that it stays molten (runny) and creates lots of volcanoes. In fact, Io is the most volcanic place in the Solar System.

From afar, Io looks like a pizza. Its colors are caused by sulfur, and the fumes contain chemicals similar to those used in stink bombs. This could also make Io the smelliest moon in the Solar System!

THIS IS JUPITER'S "PIZZA" MOON, IO. THE DARK SPOTS ARE THE CRATERS OF ACTIVE VOLCANOES.

JUPITER'S GREAT RED SPOT IS A MASSIVE HURRICANE THAT'S BEEN BLOWING FOR SEVERAL HUNDRED YEARS.

WEIRD WORLD

RADIO TELESCOPES PICK UP SIGNALS COMING FROM JUPITER, CAUSED BY STORMS AND BY CHANGES IN THE PLANET'S MAGNETIC FIELD. A COMPOSER ONCE BASED A PIECE OF MUSIC ON THE STRANGE NOISES!

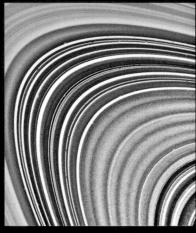

Some experts think life may exist in these dark, distant oceans.

Jupiter's other two big moons are Ganymede and Callisto. Both have icy, rocky surfaces scarred with craters and cracks. Ganymede is the largest moon in the Solar System– – bigger than the planet Mercury. Jupiter has many more, smaller moons.

The next moon out from Io is Europa, which is the size of our Moon. Its thick, cracked, icy crust is believed by scientists to cover oceans of liquid water.

SOME OF SATURN'S RINGLETS ARE NOT CIRCULAR, BUT OVAL

Europa, like Io, is squeezed and kept warm by tides caused by Jupiter's powerful gravity, which probably also causes the cracks in the ice.

Saturn – ringed wonder
Beyond Jupiter is Saturn, which is several times larger than Earth. For many people, Saturn is the most beautiful of the planets, on account of its awesome rings.

Those rings are made up of millions of orbiting chunks of rock and ice. The rings stretch more than 170,000 miles (270,000 km) across, but are only

ONE OF SATURN'S STRANGEST MOONS IS MIMAS. IT WAS NEARLY SHATTERED BY AN IMPACT. IT NOW LOOKS LIKE THE DEATH STAR FROM *STAR WARS!*

about 110 yd (100 m) thick. Sometimes, when the edges of the rings face Earth, we can't see them at all. Though Saturn

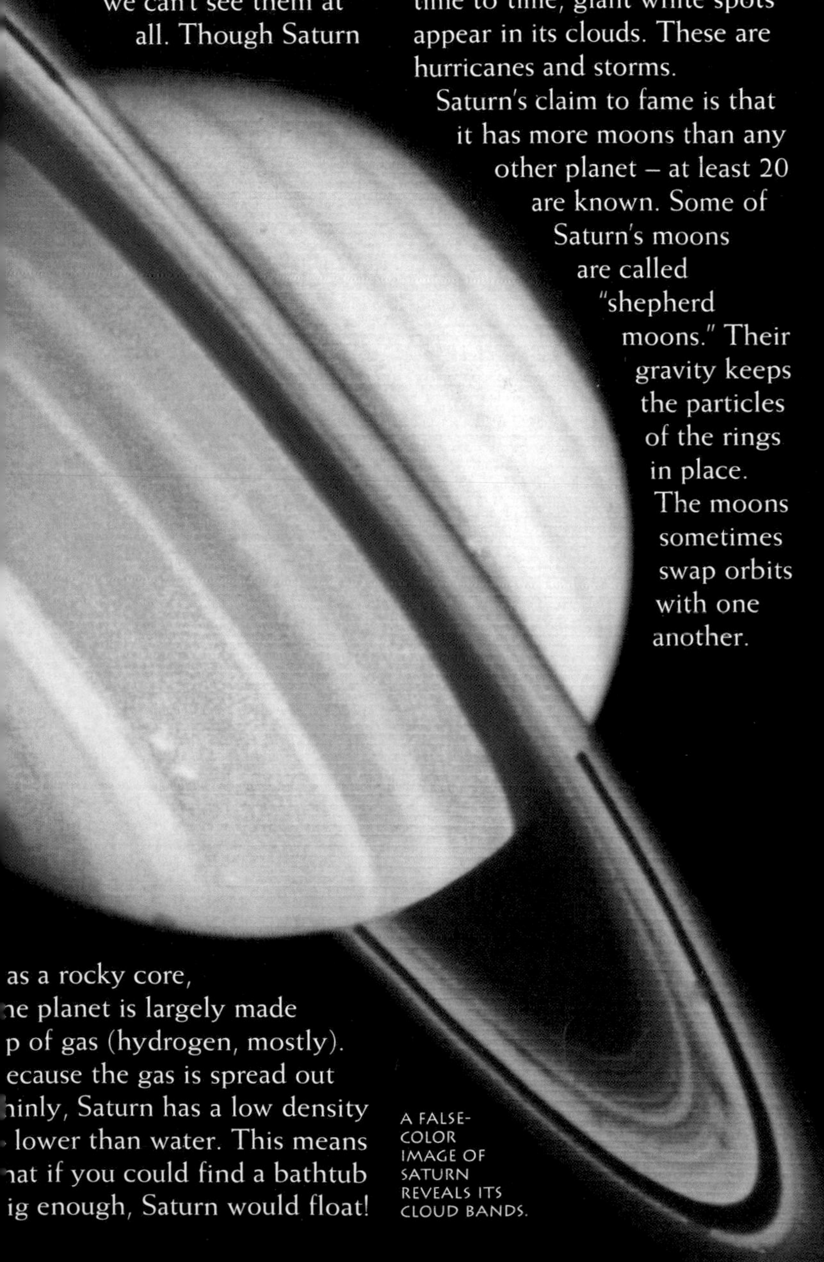

Big family

Saturn isn't as colorful as Jupiter, but it's windy. From time to time, giant white spots appear in its clouds. These are hurricanes and storms.

Saturn's claim to fame is that it has more moons than any other planet – at least 20 are known. Some of Saturn's moons are called "shepherd moons." Their gravity keeps the particles of the rings in place. The moons sometimes swap orbits with one another.

has a rocky core, the planet is largely made up of gas (hydrogen, mostly). Because the gas is spread out thinly, Saturn has a low density – lower than water. This means that if you could find a bathtub big enough, Saturn would float!

A FALSE-
COLOR
IMAGE OF
SATURN
REVEALS ITS
CLOUD BANDS.

One of the most interesting of Saturn's moons is Titan. Larger than Mercury but smaller than Ganymede, Titan just might be a young Earth in deep freeze. It has a smoggy, orange atmosphere. Scientists think there may be seas of liquid methane in which icebergs float around. In 2004, a mission named *Cassini-Huygens* is due to reach Titan. It will drop a probe onto the moon to find out more about it.

Newer planets

Beyond Saturn are Uranus and Neptune, which were unknown to the ancient astronomers. William Herschel discovered Uranus in 1781, and Neptune was only spotted in 1846. In the 1980s, the *Voyager* 2 space probe paid them a visit.

URANUS IS JUST VISIBLE TO THE NAKED EYE ON A CLEAR NIGHT

Green gas giant

Uranus is four times the size of Earth. Its thick atmosphere is made up mostly of hydrogen. It also contains methane, which gives it a green color.

THE CASSINI-HUYGENS ORBITER AND PROBE, LAUNCHED FROM THE US IN 1997, WILL STUDY SATURN AND ITS MANY RINGS, AS WELL AS MOONS SUCH AS TITAN.

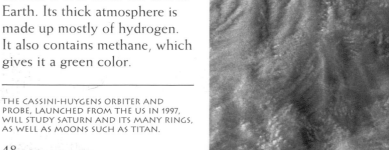

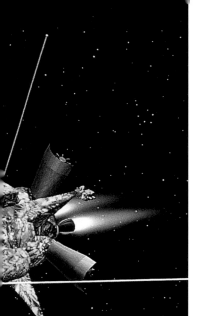

LOG ON...
See more of Saturn at
http://saturn.jpl.nasa.gov

Just like Saturn, Uranus has rings, but they are coal black. Astronomers found the rings in 1977 by watching a nearby star. They saw it "wink" in and out behind the rings before disappearing behind Uranus.

Rolling around

Uranus has quite a few moons, and they are all named after characters from Shakespeare's plays. One of the most unusual is Miranda, which appears to have been broken apart,

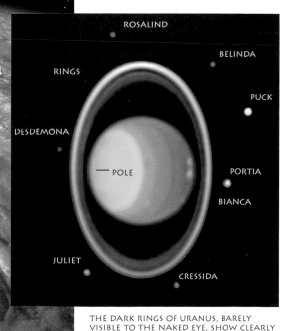

ROSALIND

BELINDA

RINGS

PUCK

DESDEMONA

— POLE

PORTIA

BIANCA

JULIET

CRESSIDA

THE DARK RINGS OF URANUS, BARELY VISIBLE TO THE NAKED EYE, SHOW CLEARLY IN A FALSE-COLOR PHOTO. EIGHT OF ITS MOONS CAN ALSO BE SEEN.

49

perhaps by a colliding asteroid. The moon's gravity pulled it back together again! It has huge cliffs more than 10 miles (16 km) high.

PLUTO

Scientists think that long ago, something else struck Uranus, knocking the planet on its side. This means that the planet's poles point toward the Sun, so that at times it appears to roll around the Sun instead of spinning around like a top, as the other planets do. If you lived on Uranus, you'd have 42 years of daylight, then 42 years of darkness – the longest night in the Solar System!

Neptune

Neptune is slightly smaller than Uranus and is a similar greenish color, but it has some truly surprising features. Violent storms in Neptune's atmosphere show up as large dark blotches and white spots. Streaky white clouds hang in the atmosphere.

Some of Neptune's winds have been measured at more than 1,300 mph (2,080 kmh). These are about 10 times more powerful than our fiercest hurricanes on Earth, which look like a gentle breeze by comparison!

WEIRD WORLD
FROM TIME TO TIME, PLUTO COMES CLOSER TO THE SUN THAN NEPTUNE. BETWEEN 1979 AND 1999, FOR EXAMPLE, NEPTUNE WAS THE FARTHEST PLANET FROM THE SUN.

TRITON IS NEPTUNE'S LARGEST MOON. THE BLACK STREAKS ARE THE NITROGEN GEYSERS THAT ERUPT ON ITS SURFACE.

A PHOTOGRAPH TAKEN BY VOYAGER 2 SHOWS NEPTUNE LOOKING MORE BLUISH THAN GREENISH

50

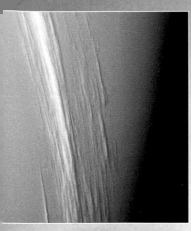

THESE WHITE STREAKS ARE CLOUDS
LYING ABOUT 25 MILES (40 KM) ABOVE
NEPTUNE'S MAIN CLOUD LAYERS.

Neptune's winds were measured by *Voyager 2*, which took 12 years to reach the planet. *Voyager 2* also found that Neptune has rings. These are coal black, like those around Uranus, and collisions between small moons may have contributed to the rings.

Astronomers once thought that the rings didn't go all the way around the planet, but *Voyager 2* showed that they do.

Cold and pink

The largest of Neptune's eight moons is Triton. This is the coldest place on record in the Solar System, with recorded temperatures of -455 °F (-235 °C). Triton's orbit will one day take it so close to Neptune that gravity will break it up.

Photographs of Triton show that nitrogen geysers spout through its icy surface. The eruptions create dark streaks across the pink surface.

Odd one out

Beyond Neptune is not another gassy planet, but a world that some people think is too small to call a planet. Pluto was discovered in 1930 and named (after the Roman god of the Underworld) by a 13-year-old girl from Oxford, England.

Although it is smaller than many moons, Pluto does have a moon of its own – Charon. No spacecraft has yet visited them, and the best pictures are still rather fuzzy. Astronomers think that they are made of rock and ice.

Pluto may be the largest member of a group of rocky, icy bodies right at the very edge of the Solar System. This group is named the Edgeworth-Kuiper Belt, after the scientists who predicted its existence. A large number of Kuiper Belt objects have been found in recent years.

THIS SPOT, A MAJOR HURRICANE OBSERVED
BY VOYAGER 2, WAS NAMED THE GREAT
DARK SPOT. IT WAS GONE BY THE TIME
THE HUBBLE TELESCOPE LOOKED FOR IT.

SPACE ROCKS

Watch out – asteroid ahead! While it might be science fiction to steer through a deadly jumble of asteroids in a starfighter, there really is an asteroid belt in our Solar System. There are also lots of other bits of rock, ice, and dust lurking out there – pieces of debris left over from the birth of the Solar System. Some of them create pretty effects in the night sky, while others could be very dangerous.

LOG ON...
See space rocks at
www.nearearthobjects.co.uk

The asteroid belt

Between Mars and Jupiter lies a band of rocks known as the Asteroid Belt. Most are roughly shaped and range from the size of a pebble to nearly 625 miles (1,000 km) across.

More than 5,000 of the largest asteroids have been found. All told, there may be millions. People once thought that asteroids were the remains they are made of.

One asteroid, named Ida, was found to have its own tiny moon.

In movies, asteroids are shown close together, but in reality they're spread thinly across the belt. If you flew close to one, you probably wouldn't see any others.

ASTEROIDS CALLED TROJANS ORBIT IN THE SAME PATH AS JUPITER

of a smashed-up planet. But there isn't enough rock. If you collected it all, it would only equal the size of a small moon.

Not all asteroids are made purely of rock. Some contain carbon or metals, and there are many different types. Spacecraft have visited a couple of asteroids to find out what

A VIEW OF OUR SOLAR SYSTEM SHOWS THE ASTEROID BELT BETWEEN MARS AND JUPITER AND A VISITING COMET.

Numbers and names

When it is discovered, an asteroid is given a catalog number. Once astronomers know its orbit, the discoverer may get to name it. Ceres, the first asteroid to be discovered, was found in 1801.

Hairy stars

Asteroids aren't much to look at, though. Star-watchers spot them in their telescopes as faint points of light. For something spectacular, you need to look for a comet. Comet is a word that comes from the Greek *kometes*, which means "hairy" and refers to the comet's tail.

Comets are dirty snowballs, a few miles (km) across. They go around the Sun in elliptical (long, rather than circular) orbits. This means they spend most of their time a long way from the Sun, where it's cold and their ice stays frozen. When they near the Sun, the ice heats up and turns to a gas. A huge "tail" then appears, made up of the gases and dust from the

on a comet – some made up of dust, and a fainter bluish tail of gas. We can see the dust tails because the dust reflects the Sun's light, just as dust in a room sparkles in a sunbeam.

WEIRD WORLD
IN 1910, EARTH PASSED THROUGH THE TAIL OF HALLEY'S COMET. TRICKSTERS SOLD "COMET PILLS" TO PEOPLE WHO THOUGHT THEY MIGHT GET SICK, AND OTHERS SOLD "COMET WINE"!

Space dust
As comets orbit the Sun, the dust from their tails is added to the debris left

AS WELL AS THE LONG, STREAMING DUST TAIL, YOU CAN SEE THE SEPARATE GAS TAIL OF THIS COMET. IT'S A BLUISH COLOR.

comet. Comet tails can be hundreds of millions of miles (km) long, but a jarful of "comet tail" would contain only a couple of specks of dust!

Light and particles from the Sun push the comet tail so that it always streams away from the Sun. You may see several tails

over from when our Solar System was formed. Every day, specks of space dust fall toward Earth – more than 25,000 tons of it each year!

Most of this dust vanishes in our atmosphere as a result of friction. Air rubs against the dust as it falls rapidly towards the ground. All this rubbing heats it up, and eventually it burns away. Friction would also

A TIME-LAPSE PHOTO SHOWS "SHOOTING STARS" CAUSED BY SPECKS OF DUST AS THEY BURN UP IN THE ATMOSPHERE.

cause the Space Shuttle and other spacecraft to burn up on their return to Earth if they didn't have protective shields.

S hooting stars

If this dust falls at night, you may see it burning up in a streak of light known as a shooting star or meteor. On a clear night, you can see several in an hour. Better still are meteor showers, which occur when Earth passes through one of the trails or clumps of dust left by a comet. Then you can see dozens, or even hundreds, of shooting stars – like a firework display!

THIS STONY METEORITE WAS HEATED SO MUCH ON ITS JOURNEY THROUGH THE ATMOSPHERE THAT IT STARTED TO MELT. ITS SURFACE STILL BEARS THE SCARS.

55

called "irons." Stony-iron meteorites contain both rock and metal. Most meteorites come from the asteroids, but scientists find a few from the Moon or, even more rarely, Mars.

Rocks from space
Occasionally, rocks fall toward Earth. Most burn up, but if a piece was big to start with,

Impact!
A meteorite the size of a soccer ball will do little damage. No one has yet been killed by a meteorite, although cars and houses have been damaged.

METEORITES STRIKE AT SEVERAL TIMES THE SPEED OF SOUND

there might be enough to land. We call this a meteorite.

Meteorites made of rock are usually called "stones," and those made of metal are

Astronomers do look out for much bigger pieces of rock because they can be a serious problem. Something less than 55 yd (50 m) across will usually get

THE METEORITE THAT STRUCK 65 MILLION YEARS AGO, AND COULD HAVE WIPED OUT THE DINOSAURS, WAS ABOUT 10 KM (6 MILES) IN DIAMETER.

burned up on the way to the ground. But a rock up to about 1,100 yd (1 km) across would survive to strike the ground and wipe out a city. Luckily, space is very big. As a result, rocks this size don't come along very often, perhaps once every few hundred years.

We can see the scars on Earth caused by previous bits of rock hitting us. Some scientists think the dinosaurs could have been wiped out when an enormous meteorite crashed through the atmosphere some 65 million years ago and struck Central America. Its impact would have thrown up enough dust to block light from the Sun for many years, killing off plants.

Space debris

Not all objects burning up in Earth's atmosphere, or crash-landing from space, are pieces of rock. Over the last 40 years, we have put many satellites and spacecraft into space. Circling our planet are parts from old satellites, rockets, and even the odd space tool or piece of space garbage that has been left up there by astronauts or cosmonauts. Sometimes it's this assorted stuff you see burning up as it falls to Earth.

In space, these pieces collide and break into smaller pieces. These may not sound deadly, but because objects in space travel faster than a bullet, they can be a problem.

GALAXIES

Our Sun and all the stars you can see in the night sky are part of a giant "star city" or galaxy, which we call the Milky Way. It's made up of billions of stars. But stars are the only things in our Galaxy. Among other features, the Milky Way is home to giant clusters of stars, black holes, and clouds of dust and gas. Some of these glow, while others are dark. Galaxies come in all shapes and sizes, and ours is just one in possibly millions.

River of stars

On a clear night you can see a hazy band of light forming a snakelike trail across the sky. Ancient people thought it was a great river in the sky, or perhaps the milk spilled from the breast of a goddess. They called it the Milky Way.

If you look carefully at the fuzzy band through a pair of binoculars, you'll notice that it certainly isn't a river! In fact, it's made up of millions of stars. Astronomers now know that when you gaze at the Milky Way, you are looking along the disk toward the center of our Galaxy.

Dirty view

You can't see every star in our Galaxy, though. This is because dust gets in the way. Just as dirt

THIS ARTIST'S IMPRESSION SHOWS HOW
OUR MILKY WAY MIGHT LOOK FROM
FAR AWAY. OLD YELLOW STARS
CLUSTER IN THE CENTER, AND
YOUNG BLUE STARS MARK OUT
THE SPIRAL ARMS.

listening to the radio!) With the use of these radio waves, astronomers are able to map the rest of our Galaxy and look at its spiral arms.

An outside view

If we could leave our Galaxy and look back at it, we'd see that it looked rather like two fried eggs laid back to back. The middle bulge (the "yolk") is made up of ancient stars. A flat disk surrounding it (the "white") contains lots of dust, gas, and stars. The dust and gas form the great "arms" that spiral outwards from the middle. From above, the Milky Way would look like a giant pinwheel.

You are here

Our Sun lies about two-thirds of the way out from the center to the edge of the disk, between two spiral arms. The stars closest to us in space are the ones that we see in the night sky.

on a windowpane blocks the view of what's beyond, so the clouds of dust in our Galaxy stop us from seeing across to the other side.

But while light can't make it far through the dust, radio waves from space can. (A dirty window doesn't stop you from

The Sun, the planets, and all the other stars are moving through space as they orbit the Milky Way. It takes about 250 million years for our Sun to complete one orbit. We might call that a galactic year.

But you don't see the stars whizzing across the night sky. The distances between them are so vast that you would need to wait hundreds of thousands of years to see much difference! If an astronomer from Ancient Greece traveled 2,000 years forward in time to the present day, he might just be able to spot that one or two stars had moved a very tiny amount.

IN THIS CLOUD OF GAS AND DUST IN THE MILKY WAY, STARS ARE BEING BORN. THE STARS GLOW PINK AND BLUE, AND THE DUST SHOWS UP AS DARK PATCHES

S tar nurseries

There are many huge and beautiful clouds of gas in the disk of our Galaxy. They're places where new stars are being born. As the stars "switch on," they light up the rest of the gas and make it glow.

Gas that is lit up in this way glows a pinkish color. If there is dust in the cloud, then it glows a bluish color, just as dust in Earth's atmosphere scatters sunlight and makes the sky look blue.

S tar traffic jams

Most of these star-forming clouds are in the spiral arms of the Galaxy. Astronomers think that this is because the spiral arms are formed by the dust and gas bunching up as it travels around the Galaxy.

It's rather like the way traffic on a busy road bunches up and slows down, and then moves freely again a little later. This cosmic "bunching" helps to compress the clouds of gas, triggering their collapse into stars and planets.

A LONG-EXPOSURE PHOTO (IN WHICH THE SHUTTER IS LEFT OPEN FOR A LONG TIME) SHOWS THE MILKY WAY AT NIGHT. YOU CAN SEE QUITE CLEARLY THE CLOUDS OF GAS AND THE DARK SMUDGES OF DUST.

Weird World

Clouds of alcohol exist in space. One cloud holds enough for 1 quart (1 liter) of beer a day for every adult in the world for the next 300 trillion years!

THE OMEGA CENTAURI GLOBULAR CLUSTER IS A BALL OF ABOUT 100,000 ANCIENT STARS. IT CIRCLES OUR GALAXY AT A DISTANCE OF ABOUT 17,000 LIGHT-YEARS.

S ticking together

A cloud of gas and dust can produce many stars. The new stars stay together for a while, but the cluster eventually drifts apart. This is because each star moves through space in its own particular way.

You could think of the stars like runners on a racetrack. They are all running at different speeds, so it's no surprise that some eventually pull out in front while others lag behind.

Once upon a time, our Sun would have been close to the stars it was born with – but that was about 5 billion years ago. The 20 or so "laps" of the Galaxy that our Sun has done since then have given the stars plenty of time to split up.

Our Galaxy contains many star clusters, each containing from a few dozen to a few hundred stars. Sometimes the cluster is still surrounded by the gas from which it was born.

G lobular clusters

Circling around the outside of our Galaxy, rather like a swarm of bees, are the globular clusters. These are giant balls of stars, each containing as many as 100,000 stars.

Scientists think that globular clusters formed very early on in the history of the Galaxy, and that these stars may, therefore, be some of the oldest in the

Universe. The brightest of the clusters, some of which give out the equivalent light of more than a million suns, appear to us as fuzzy "stars" in the night sky.

There is no dust or gas in these clusters for forming new stars. If you lived on a planet orbiting a star in a globular cluster, you would have a night sky that was packed with stars and almost as bright as day!

But just imagine the view from a planet orbiting a star on the very edge of the cluster. When you looked into space, you'd see the whole Galaxy in all its majesty. Awesome!

Clouds

If you go to the southern hemisphere and look up on a really clear night, you will see two other fuzzy patches of light that look like bits of the Milky Way that have been torn off. The Portuguese explorer Ferdinand Magellan (1480–1521) first noticed these during a voyage around the world, so we call them the Magellanic Clouds.

They aren't clouds at all, but small, irregular galaxies that go around our Milky Way at a distance of 150–200,000 light years. The Large Magellanic Cloud has gas and dust clouds and star clusters of its own.

LOG ON..
http://stardate.org/
resources/galaxy

GLOBULAR STAR CLUSTERS MAY BE MORE THAN 12 BILLION YEARS OLD

The Small Magellanic Cloud seems to have used up most of its gas and dust and is just made up of lots of stars.

Astronomers studying the Milky Way have detected that there were once other satellite galaxies, but over time, they have merged with ours. In

THESE FUZZY PATCHES OF LIGHT ARE THE MAGELLANIC CLOUDS – A COUPLE OF SMALL GALAXIES ORBITING THE MILKY WAY.

63

time, it's probable that the Magellanic Clouds will also end up becoming just a part of the Milky Way.

Groups of galaxies

Our Galaxy won't reign supreme forever. It's part of a small cluster of galaxies called the Local Group. There are three large, spiral-shaped galaxies in the Local Group, as well as several smaller, blob-shaped galaxies.

The nearest spiral galaxy is called the Andromeda Galaxy, and it's about twice the size of the Milky Way. It's a long way away. Light takes about 2 million years to get there.

But this galaxy is moving slowly toward us, and in the very distant future, it will begin to merge with the Milky Way.

TWO GALAXIES MERGE. THOUGH STARS SELDOM COLLIDE, SUCH AN ENCOUNTER CAN PULL A GALAXY APART.

THE ANDROMEDA GALAXY IS THE CLOSEST GALAXY TO OUR OWN. ONE DAY IT WILL MERGE WITH THE MILKY WAY.

Bizarrely, because galaxies are mostly empty space, there will probably be no actual collisions between stars!

Shapes and sizes

There are billions of other galaxies in the Universe, and they come in all shapes and

sizes. Spiral galaxies, like our Milky Way and Andromeda, may be tightly wound with lots of arms, or very loose with just a few arms. There are elliptical galaxies that look like balls.

think that this is because they have active black holes in their centers.

When we look out into very deep space, we see that galaxies are gathered in clusters, and

Some are round, and others look more like footballs. Then there are irregular galaxies. These are shapeless galaxies that have been torn apart by a close encounter with another galaxy.

THIS TINY SECTION OF DEEP SPACE SHOWS THAT THE UNIVERSE CONTAINS A VAST NUMBER OF GALAXIES.

then into superclusters. There doesn't seem to be much in the space between the galaxies or clusters, but scientists suspect that "dark matter" may be

Active galaxies

Some of the most interesting galaxies in the Universe are active galaxies. These are sending out massive jets of radiation and they are very bright. Astronomers

lurking out there. No one is quite sure what goes into making dark matter, but it may consist of tiny particles left over from the Big Bang.

WEIRD WORLD

ONE OF THE LARGEST KNOWN GALAXIES IS M87, IN THE CONSTELLATION OF VIRGO. CONTAINING TRILLIONS OF STARS, IT IS THOUGHT TO HOUSE A GIANT BLACK HOLE.

THE BIG BANG

The problem with the beginning of the Universe is that no one was there to see it. So answering the really important question of how it all began is difficult. Scientists have to take a look at the Universe and, like detectives, weigh up the evidence to work out how it got to be that way. There are lots of different ideas, but only one theory that fits most of the clues. Astronomers call it the Big Bang.

Vanishing galaxies

Many people in the past had ideas about the Universe. Some of those ideas were based on what they saw in the Universe, and others on religious or mythological points of view.

But in the 1920s an American scientist named Edwin Hubble noticed something about the distant fuzzy patches of light, called galaxies, that he was looking at. They all seemed to be moving away from us.

But why? Is this because our Galaxy is the worst place to be in the Universe?

Cosmic cooking

Hubble's answer to this puzzle was that the Universe must be expanding. Wherever you were in the Universe, everything would seem to be moving away from you.

This is tricky to get your head around, so think of the Universe like a cake mix with raisins in it. As the cake bakes, it expands, pushing the raisins apart. No matter which raisin you looked at, it would seem as if all the other raisins were moving away from it. The raisins aren't moving through the cake – it's the cake between them that is expanding.

That's just like the Universe. The galaxies are moving apart, not because they are flying through space, but because the space itself is stretching!

In the beginning

So if the Universe is now expanding, was there a time in the past when it was all

THE BIG BANG INVOLVED A TRULY MASSIVE AMOUNT OF ENERGY. NO ONE CAN REALLY IMAGINE WHAT IT MUST HAVE BEEN LIKE.

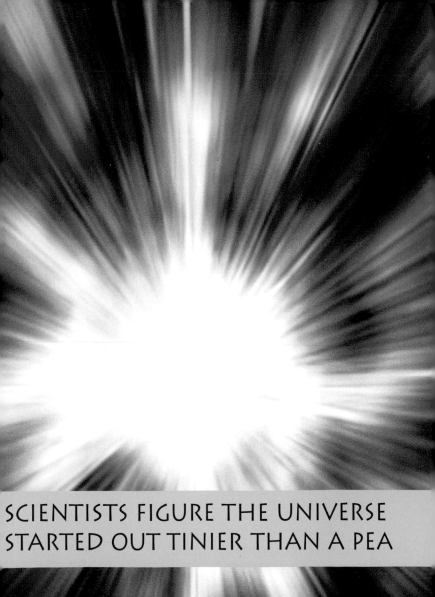

SCIENTISTS FIGURE THE UNIVERSE
STARTED OUT TINIER THAN A PEA

SCIENTISTS USE SEVERAL SUPERCOMPUTERS LINKED TOGETHER IN THEIR ATTEMPTS TO UNDERSTAND THE BIG BANG.

was a problem on the ground, and even had workmen clean out all the pigeon nests that were on the telescope. But still the hiss remained.

One day, while they were talking to another astronomer about the problem, they realized that this hiss must be the afterglow of

squished up together? And did some kind of massive explosion, a Big Bang, take place to cause it all to expand?

Afterglow
Astronomers thought long and hard about the problem of the Universe expanding. They worked out that if the Universe did begin from a single point, then we should be able to detect the glow of that original cosmic fireball.

In 1965, two American astronomers called Arno Penzias and Robert Wilson were working with a radio telescope (a telescope that looks at radio waves coming from space). The telescope kept picking up an annoying hiss, which seemed to be everywhere. They thought it

that original mighty explosion. Hearing the Big Bang's "echo" helped convince astronomers that they were on the right track with their ideas.

Boom!
So now we know that the Universe probably began about 12 billion years ago, from

nothing. It's hard to imagine nothing. Something happened – and we don't know what – to make a small "seed" of the Universe suddenly inflate and expand, creating all the matter and energy we have today. It sounds like science fiction, but it really happened!

A MAP OF THE WHOLE SKY TAKEN BY THE COBE SATELLITE SHOWS THE TINY VARIATIONS THAT RESULTED FROM THE BIG BANG EXPLOSION. PINK IS HOTTER THAN BLUE.

In the mix

The Big Bang is a detective story that astronomers are still working on. They use very powerful computers to try to recreate the Universe from a "recipe" based on their other observations. Astronomers feed in the ingredients, tell the computer how to put it all together, and then fast-forward their new universe by 12 billion years and see whether their result looks anything like the real Universe!

Big Crunch

But how will it all end? The equations tell us that there are two possible endings for the Universe. It may go on expanding forever. Or, if there is enough matter in the Universe, gravity will eventually start pulling it all back together, and maybe everything will end in a Big Crunch.

At the moment it looks as if there isn't enough matter in the Universe to cause a Big Crunch. However, experts are finding all kinds of weird "dark matter" and "dark energy." Some of them think that as we find out more about our Universe, we will discover enough matter to stop it from expanding forever.

WEIRD WORLD
THE NAME "BIG BANG" WAS FIRST COINED BY BRITISH ASTRONOMER SIR FRED HOYLE, WHO DIDN'T BELIEVE THE THEORY AND USED THE PHRASE TO MAKE FUN OF IT.

DO ALIENS EXIST?

Are we alone? With all that space, all those stars, all those planets, it's really hard to believe that we are the only form of life in the Universe. But we haven't made contact – yet. Until we do, scientists must rely on what is known about life on Earth to try and imagine how it might also happen out there...

THE BEAGLE 2 PROBE ATTACHED TO MARS EXPRESS WILL VISIT THE RED PLANET IN 2003 TO LOOK FOR SIGNS THAT LIFE MAY ONCE HAVE EXISTED THERE.

Close to home

In our search for life in the Universe, we may as well begin with what we know. Earth, of course, provides the right conditions. But from what we know about life, could it exist on other planets in our Solar System?

Scientists think life will need liquid water, which allows the chemistry that bodies need. Life will also need an energy source. We rely on sunlight for energy, but it's not the only source. There are creatures living near volcanic vents on the dark ocean floor that survive on sulfur, rather than sunlight. Life on Earth appears in weird places!

Looking at the nine planets in our Solar System,

we can probably rule out
Mercury because it is too hot
and has no water, and Venus
likewise is too toasty. But
what about Mars?

Martians

In the 19th century
people got excited
about the possibility
of life on Mars.
They thought it
was a dying world,
and that Martians
were building canals
to transport water
from the polar icecaps
to the dry plains.

We now know that
this was just fanciful
thinking. But the
spacecraft we have
sent to Mars show that
it once was much
warmer and wetter there.
And recently, spacecraft
have sent back images
showing that in places there
may still be liquid water
bubbling up to the surface.

Hope in microbes

Some astronomers believe that
tiny shapes in a meteorite from
Mars are fossils of microbes,
showing that perhaps life did
get started there long ago.

But is life still there? In 2003
and 2004 several spacecraft are
heading for Mars in search of

HOLLYWOOD
ALIENS OFTEN
SEEM HUMANOID
(HUMANLIKE). BUT
WOULD THEY LOOK
LIKE THIS?

an answer to that question. Even if they only find fossil microbes, it would prove that conditions were once right for life on Mars. And that would prove that life on Earth may not be a one-time happening.

Watery worlds

Other places in our Solar System that have liquid water include some of the moons of Jupiter. Europa is believed

to have an ocean trapped under an icy crust several miles thick. The ocean is heated by the tides that Jupiter causes. It may be home to very basic life-forms or – who knows – to creatures resembling giant jellyfish.

Hunting planets

The rest of the Solar System doesn't look too promising, but planets orbiting other stars are being discovered all the time. At the moment, scientific instruments can find only big, Jupiter-sized worlds, but space telescopes are being planned that will seek Earthlike worlds.

A suitable star

If aliens exist, we might expect to find them on a planet orbiting a star of similar size to our Sun. This is because it takes billions of years for life to evolve (develop) from

MAYBE WE'LL FIND ALIENS THAT ARE PART SQUISHY, PART THINKING MACHINE.

THERE'S NO REASON WHY AN ALIEN FROM A WATERY WORLD COULDN'T BE LIKE A HUGE JELLYFISH.

Little green men
If aliens do exist, what would they look like? Probably not much like us. Just think about all the living things on Earth, and all the different forms they take. Nevertheless, if we expect these aliens to want to contact us, then they'll need to be reasonably intelligent life-forms. So we can apply a few basic laws of physics, biology, and engineering to alien evolution, and then take a guess.

simple creatures into beings as complex as us. If our Sun had been bigger, it would have used up its fuel and died ages ago, leaving too little time for humans to evolve. The same might be true of life on another planet – it would need time to evolve into a complex life-form.

Size matters
For a start, our alien won't be tiny, since a small life-form is unlikely to have enough brain cells to become intelligent.
Nor is it likely to be huge. Really big creatures need lots of energy, as well as plenty of strength to support their great weight.

WEIRD WORLD
HOLLYWOOD ALIENS VARY ACCORDING TO HOW EACH DIRECTOR WANTS YOU TO FEEL. EVIL ALIENS ARE UGLY, WHILE FRIENDLY ALIENS USUALLY LOOK LIKE CHILDREN.

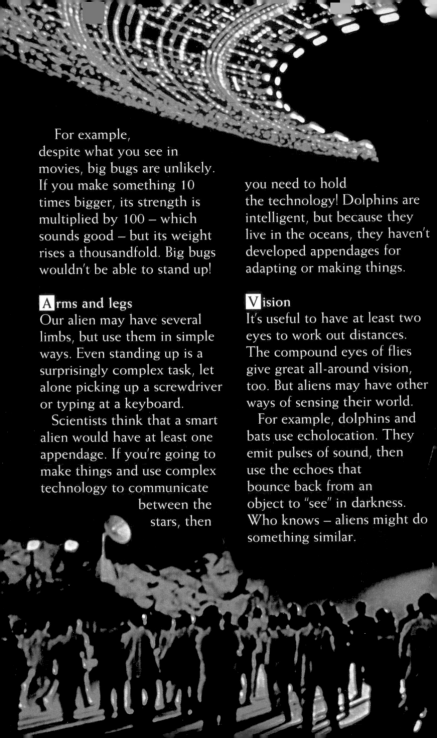

For example, despite what you see in movies, big bugs are unlikely. If you make something 10 times bigger, its strength is multiplied by 100 – which sounds good – but its weight rises a thousandfold. Big bugs wouldn't be able to stand up!

Arms and legs

Our alien may have several limbs, but use them in simple ways. Even standing up is a surprisingly complex task, let alone picking up a screwdriver or typing at a keyboard.

Scientists think that a smart alien would have at least one appendage. If you're going to make things and use complex technology to communicate between the stars, then you need to hold the technology! Dolphins are intelligent, but because they live in the oceans, they haven't developed appendages for adapting or making things.

Vision

It's useful to have at least two eyes to work out distances. The compound eyes of flies give great all-around vision, too. But aliens may have other ways of sensing their world.

For example, dolphins and bats use echolocation. They emit pulses of sound, then use the echoes that bounce back from an object to "see" in darkness. Who knows – aliens might do something similar.

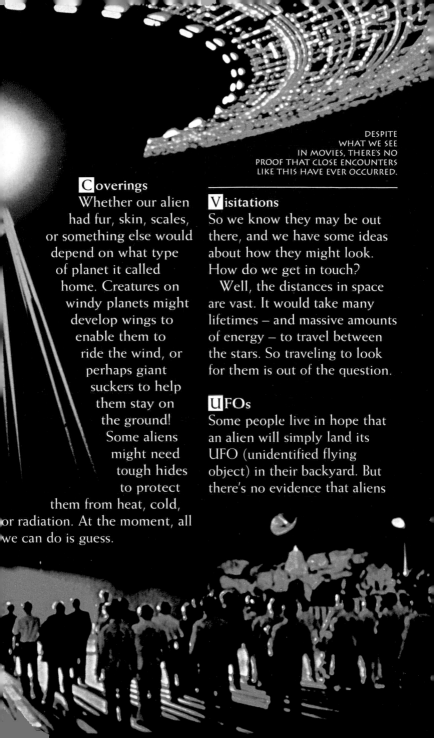

Coverings

Whether our alien had fur, skin, scales, or something else would depend on what type of planet it called home. Creatures on windy planets might develop wings to enable them to ride the wind, or perhaps giant suckers to help them stay on the ground! Some aliens might need tough hides to protect them from heat, cold, or radiation. At the moment, all we can do is guess.

Visitations

So we know they may be out there, and we have some ideas about how they might look. How do we get in touch?

Well, the distances in space are vast. It would take many lifetimes – and massive amounts of energy – to travel between the stars. So traveling to look for them is out of the question.

UFOs

Some people live in hope that an alien will simply land its UFO (unidentified flying object) in their backyard. But there's no evidence that aliens are visiting us. If there were, then scientists would be lining up to investigate!

Some people suspect that the government is covering it all up. But a look at the news shows us that most politicians are no good at keeping secrets. So, if there's a scrap of truth in rumors about alien landings, we'd know about it by now.

Getting in touch
We can't go there, and they aren't coming here. How might we discover intelligent life?

THE ARECIBO RADIO TELESCOPE IN PUERTO RICO IS THE WORLD'S LARGEST, WITH A DISH 1,000 FT (304 M) ACROSS. IT'S USED TO SEARCH FOR SIGNS OF ALIENS.

For the last 75 years or so, the powerful radio signals produced by television and the military have been leaking into space. If aliens lived within 75 light-years of Earth, and had a sensitive radio telescope, then they could pick up those signals. The signals would be unlike anything produced by nature, so the aliens would know it had to be the work of another intelligent being.

Tuning in
Scientists think that intelligent aliens – if there are any – may use radio signals to contact us. So all we have to do is use our

radio telescopes to try to tune in. Since 1960, astronomers have been doing just that.

The world's largest radio telescope is in Puerto Rico. It is used for a few weeks each year to conduct searches for extra-terrestrials. Any unusual signals are checked out by the giant Lovell Radio Telescope at Jodrell Bank in Cheshire, England. So far, all signals have been false alarms, usually just a communications satellite.

Unfortunately, we don't know where to listen on the dial, so we have to scan as much of the radio band as we can for something that can't be produced by nature. This takes time. But as computers improve, then they can do the scanning for us.

The SETI (Search for Extra-Terrestrial Intelligence) Institute, based in California, looks for alien life and conducts experiments to work out how life gets started in the Universe. They also think hard about what we would say if ET were to call!

The truth is out there…
A new telescope, the Allen Telescope Array, is being built in California. When complete, its 350 dishes will search the skies 24 hours a day. Scientists at work on this believe that if life is as plentiful as we think it might be, they may pick up a signal in the next 20–30 years.

IN 1974 THE ARECIBO TELESCOPE BEAMED A MESSAGE TO THE STARS

STAR-GAZING

The great thing about space is that you can experience it for yourself. The telescopes of professional astronomers are positioned on mountaintops to get above the clouds, or on satellites to escape the atmosphere altogether. But you already own a good astronomical instrument – your eyes! Once you know what to look for, and gather some hints and tips, you will be ready to look a little deeper into space.

A SIMPLE PAIR OF BINOCULARS WILL HELP YOU SEE OBJECTS IN THE NIGHT SKY, AND IS AN INEXPENSIVE START TO STAR-GAZING.

On a fine night...

The first thing you need for star-gazing is a clear, dark night. This is not as easy as it sounds, because most of us live in well-lit neighborhoods. A lot of the street lighting shines upward, and the glare makes it difficult to see the fainter stars.

Once you're in position, your eyes need to adjust to the dark. This takes a minute or two. Then look up!

Seeing stars

Check out the stars. If you look carefully, you may see stars of different colors.

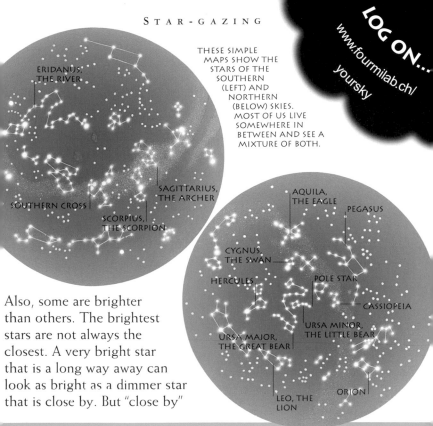

LOG ON...
www.fourmilab.ch/
yoursky

THESE SIMPLE MAPS SHOW THE STARS OF THE SOUTHERN (LEFT) AND NORTHERN (BELOW) SKIES. MOST OF US LIVE SOMEWHERE IN BETWEEN AND SEE A MIXTURE OF BOTH.

ERIDANUS, THE RIVER

SOUTHERN CROSS

SCORPIUS, THE SCORPION

SAGITTARIUS, THE ARCHER

AQUILA, THE EAGLE

PEGASUS

CYGNUS, THE SWAN

HERCULES

POLE STAR

CASSIOPEIA

URSA MINOR, THE LITTLE BEAR

URSA MAJOR, THE GREAT BEAR

ORION

LEO, THE LION

Also, some are brighter than others. The brightest stars are not always the closest. A very bright star that is a long way away can look as bright as a dimmer star that is close by. But "close by"

UNLIKE A STAR, A PLANET NEVER TWINKLES IN THE NIGHT SKY

isn't actually that close. All the stars are more than a trillion miles away!

C onnect the dots
You might want to "connect the dots" and make patterns, just as people have done for centuries. There are 88 patterns of stars, or constellations, in the night sky. Many of them are named after animals or

characters from Greek and Roman stories, such as Orion the hunter and Hercules.

A good star chart will name all the stars, and mark features of interest, such as star clusters and galaxies. To see most of these, however, you need a pair of binoculars or a telescope.

During the night, the stars change position. Just as the trees in the park seem to move around you when you ride a merry-go-round – even though you know you're spinning – the stars also appear to move around the Earth. But in reality, it's the Earth that's rotating.

It's also important to remember that, as well as rotating on its own axis, Earth is moving around the Sun. This means that you will see different patterns of stars in the sky at different times of the year.

The Moon

On many nights, you'll see the Moon in the sky. We've all noticed how sometimes it is full and round, and at other times it looks like a "C," called a crescent moon.

As the Moon orbits Earth, we see different amounts of the side lit by the Sun. These are the phases of the Moon. It takes about a month for the Moon to go through its phases.

You can try this for yourself in a darkened room. Fix a ball, such as a tennis ball, to a stick.

THESE ARE THE PHASES OF THE MOON. LEFT TO RIGHT: ALMOST NEW MOON, LAST CRESCENT, LAST QUARTER, FULL MOON, FIRST QUARTER, FIRST CRESCENT, JUST PAST NEW MOON.

This will be the Moon. Your head is Earth. Switch on a desk lamp – this can be the Sun.

Facing the lamplight, hold the ball in front of you. You see only the side of the ball that is in shadow. This is the position of a new moon. Move the ball around so that it lines up with

80

your ear. Now you can see half the lit side and half the shaded side. This is a quarter moon.

Now turn your back to the desk lamp and hold the ball in front of you. You should be able to see all of the lit side – unless your head gets in the way! This is a full moon.

shadow for a while. It doesn't happen every month because the Moon's orbit around the Earth keeps it clear of the shadow for most of the time.

If you watch a lunar eclipse, you'll see that Earth's shadow has a curved edge, proving that our planet isn't flat!

Lunar eclipses

The Latin name for a moon is *luna*, and we use this word in the term lunar eclipse. If you try the demo with the ball and lamp, then you'll see what happens when your head gets between them. You eclipse (stop light from hitting) the ball. During a lunar eclipse, the Moon moves into Earth's

Planet watching

If you are a sharp observer, you'll see that there are some "stars" that don't appear on

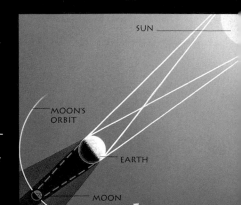

AN ECLIPSE OF THE MOON HAPPENS WHEN THE MOON MOVES INTO EARTH'S SHADOW AS IT FOLLOWS ITS ORBITAL PATH. A TOTAL ECLIPSE LASTS UP TO 100 MINUTES.

SUN

MOON'S ORBIT

EARTH

MOON

BLACK HOLES

your star charts. These are the planets. The word planet comes from a Greek word meaning "wanderer." To the ancient astronomers, the planets appeared to wander across the sky. We now know that they do this because they are orbiting the Sun.

During the year you can see different planets at different times. Some newspapers, as well as astronomy magazines, will tell you where to look for them on any given date.

Bright lights, big moons
A brilliant light in the east before sunrise or in the west after sunset is probably the planet Venus. It is the brightest object in the sky after the Sun and Moon. No wonder some people mistake Venus for a UFO!

binoculars or a small telescope, you can see the four largest moons of this giant.

Saturn looks rather like a yellow star, and

DURING A SOLAR ECLIPSE, THE MOON'S ORBITAL PATH TAKES IT IN FRONT OF THE SUN AND IT BRIEFLY BLOCKS OUT THE SUN'S DISC.

SOME PEOPLE TRAVEL THE WORLD TO SEE EVERY SOLAR ECLIPSE

Mercury is hard to see since it is never far from the Sun. Mars is very red, and when it's in the sky, it is easy to spot. Jupiter shines almost as brightly as Venus; and with

you'd need a small telescope to see the rings clearly. Uranus and Neptune also need a small telescope, but you'd have to borrow a huge telescope to see faraway Pluto.

82

Solar eclipse

From time to time the Moon passes between Earth and the Sun, and its shadow falls on Earth. This is called a solar eclipse. Since the Moon's shadow is relatively small, only a small area of Earth's surface sees the eclipse, which lasts from a few seconds to about seven minutes.

When the Moon covers the Sun completely, turning day briefly into night, this is called a total eclipse. Partial eclipses are more common. They occur when the Moon doesn't entirely cover the Sun.

Solar eclipses are exciting to watch, but you must not look directly at the Sun – it can seriously damage your eyes.

Shooting stars

At certain times of the year, Earth passes through big clouds of dust left by passing comets. As the dust falls to Earth, it burns up in the atmosphere, making "shooting stars."

The best way to watch these so-called "meteor showers" is to go outdoors, lie on a

ALWAYS USE SAFETY GLASSES TO WATCH A SOLAR ECLIPSE. STARING DIRECTLY AT THE SUN CAN BLIND YOU.

83

If you get to know the sky a little better, and decide that you really want to know more, then you can save up and buy a proper astronomical telescope. There are plenty of advertisements in astronomy magazines. If possible, visit a store that specializes in astronomy, because there are some telescopes on the market that are more suitable for bird-watching than planet-watching!

S ensible star-gazing

Before you go out, remember to dress warmly. It can get cold standing around staring at the sky, so a hat, gloves, and warm socks are vital. Take a flashlight, but place some red plastic wrap over it so that the beam doesn't spoil your night vision once you're used to the dark. But the most important thing is to be safe. Always go star-gazing with friends, and tell an adult where you are going and what time you will be back. Clear skies!

reclining lawn chair, cover up with a blanket, and look up at the sky.

A closer look

If you get hooked on astronomy, you may want to buy a telescope. It's usually best to start off with a good pair of binoculars and a sturdy tripod to put them on. This way you can use them for other things, and they are easy to carry around.

THIS AVERAGE AMATEUR TELESCOPE HAS A STURDY MOUNT THAT ENABLES IT TO TRACK THE STARS.

REFERENCE SECTION

Whether you've finished reading *Black Holes*, or are turning to this section first, you'll find the information on the next eight pages really helpful. Here are all the astronomical facts and figures, background details, and unfamiliar words you'll need to get started. You'll also find a useful list of website addresses – so, whether you want to surf the net or search out facts, these pages should turn you from an enthusiast into an expert.

OUR SOLAR SYSTEM

SOLAR SYSTEM FACTS

• Nine planets orbit our closest star, the Sun. Four (Mercury, Venus, Earth, and Mars) are rocky, four (Jupiter, Saturn, Uranus, and Neptune) are gas giants, and one (Pluto) is a world of rock and ice.

• Jupiter, the largest planet in our Solar System, could hold 1,300 Earths.

• Saturn has the most moons of any planet – at least 20 (and there may be more to be found).

• Uranus has a 42-year "summer," followed by a 42-year "winter."

	Distance from Sun million miles (km)	Diameter miles (km)	Temperature °F (°C)	Time taken to turn on axis (Earth days)	Time taken to orbit Sun (Earth days/years)	Number of rings	Number of moons
Mercury	36.0 (57.9)	3,031 (4,878)	−292/+806 (−180/+430)	58 days, 16 hours	87.97 days	0	0
Venus	67.2 (108.2)	7,520 (12,103)	869 (465)	243 days, 14 minutes	224.70 days	0	0
Earth	93 (149.6)	7,926 (12,756)	−94/+131 (−70/+55)	23 hours, 56 minutes	365.26 days	0	1
Mars	141,6 (227.9)	4,217 (6,786)	−184/+77 (−120/+25)	24 hours, 37 minutes	686.98 days	0	2
Jupiter	483.6 (778.3)	88,846 (142,984)	−238 (−150)	9 hours, 55 minutes	11.86 years	3	16
Saturn	886 (1,427)	74,898 (120,536)	−292 (−180)	10 hours, 40 minutes	29.46 years	7	20
Uranus	1,784 (2,871)	31,763 (51,118)	−346 (−210)	17 hours, 14 minutes	84.01 years	11	18
Neptune	2,794 (4,497)	30,775 (49,528)	−346 (−210)	16 hours, 7 minutes	164.79 years	6	8
Pluto	3,675 (5,914)	1,419 (2,284)	−364 (−220)	6 days, 9 hours	248.54 years	0	1

THE SUN

Age	5 billion years
Diameter	865,000 miles (1,392,000 km)
Mass (Earth = 1)	332,946
Distance from Earth	92.9 million miles (149.6 million km)
Distance from nearest star	24.9 trillion miles (40 trillion km)
Core temperature	25.2 million °F (14 million °C)
Surface temperature	9,900 °F (5,500 °C)
Luminosity (light power)	390 billion billion megawatts
Speed	240 million years to orbit the galaxy
Life expectancy	5 billion more years

SUN FACTS

• There are many trillions of stars in the Universe, varying in temperature and color. Our Sun is a yellow star, of average size and temperature.
• In one second, the Sun gives out 35 million times the average annual electricity supply for the entire United States.

STARS

FACTS AND RECORDS

Star numbers
The average galaxy has 100 billion stars. Our Galaxy has 200 billion.

Faintest known star
Brown star RC 0058.8-2807 has a visual brightness less than one-millionth that of the Sun.

Brightest known supernova
SN 1006 flared in April 1006. It was easily visible during the day.

Fastest known pulsar
PSR 1937+214 spins 642 times a second.

NEAREST STARS TO SUN

Star	Distance (light-years)
Proxima Centauri	4.2
Alpha Centauri A	4.3
Alpha Centauri B	4.3
Barnard's Star	5.9
Wolf 359	7.6
Lalande 21185	8.1

BRIGHTEST STARS

Star	Distance (light-years)
Sirius A	8.6
Canopus	200
Alpha Centauri	4.3
Arcturus	36
Vega	26
Capella	42

ASTRONOMICAL DISCOVERIES

335–323 BC
Aristotle (384–322 BC), Greek philosopher and physicist, claims Earth is at center of Universe.

AD 137–145
Ptolemy (c.120–180), Greco-Egyptian astronomer, sorts 1,080 stars into 48 constellations. Supports Aristotle's Earth-centered theory.

1543
Nicolaus Copernicus (1473–1543), Polish monk, establishes position of Sun at center of known Universe.

1596
Tycho Brahe (1546–1601), Danish nobleman, publishes star catalog giving positions for about 770 stars.

1608
Hans Lippershey (1570–1619), Dutch scientist, credited with inventing first telescope.

1609
Johannes Kepler (1571–1630), German astronomer, establishes that planets follow elliptical, rather than circular, orbits.

1610
Galileo Galilei (1564–1642), Italian scientist, makes first regular use of astronomical telescope.

1667
Isaac Newton (1642–1727), English scientist, launches modern science of astrophysics with his laws of gravity.

1781
William Herschel (1738–1822), German-born amateur astronomer, discovers Uranus, later finding four of its moons. He also catalogs many clusters and nebulae, and points to existence of other galaxies.

1907
Albert Einstein (1879–1955), German-born physicist, discovers mass can turn into energy. This leads to theory of how Sun shines.

1924–30
Belgian Abbé Lemaitre (1894–1966) and Russian Aleksandr Friedmann (1888–1925) independently formulate Big Bang theory.

1929
Edwin Hubble (1889–1953), American astronomer, finds evidence for an expanding Universe.

1965
Arno Penzias (b.1933) and Robert Wilson (b.1936), Americans, discover what they believe to be radiation "afterglow" of the Big Bang.

1992
COBE, Cosmic Background Explorer, sends back images of early Universe.

1995
Michael Mayor and Didier Queloz of the Geneva Observatory, Switzerland, discover first planet going around another sun-like star.

SPACE "FIRSTS"

October 4, 1957 Soviet Union launches *Sputnik 1*, world's first artificial satellite.

November 3, 1957 Laika, a dog on board *Sputnik 2*, is first living creature in space.

January 31, 1958 Launch of first US satellite, *Explorer 1*.

April 12, 1961 Cosmonaut (Soviet astronaut) Yuri Gagarin is first person in space.

February 20, 1962 John Glenn is first US astronaut to orbit Earth.

July 10, 1962 US *Telstar 1*, first communications satellite, launched.

June 16, 1963 Soviet cosmonaut Valentina Tereshkova becomes first woman in space.

March 18, 1965 Soviet cosmonaut Alexei Leonov takes first space walk outside spacecraft.

February 3, 1966 Soviet craft *Luna 9* (unmanned) makes first successful Moon landing.

October 18, 1967 Soviet *Venera 4* is first craft to land on Venus.

July 20, 1969 US astronauts Neil Armstrong and Edwin "Buzz" Aldrin are first humans to walk on Moon.

April 19, 1971 Soviets launch *Salyut 1*, world's first space station.

December 5, 1973 US craft *Pioneer 10* makes first flyby of Jupiter.

July 17, 1975 First space docking of US and Soviet craft (*Apollo–Soyuz*).

July 20, 1976 US craft *Viking 1* makes first successful Mars landing.

September 1, 1979 US craft *Pioneer 11* makes first flyby of Saturn.

April 12, 1981 First launch of US space shuttle *Columbia*.

January 24, 1986 US craft *Voyager 2* makes first flyby of Uranus.

February 20, 1986 Launch of Soviet *Mir* space station.

March 14, 1986 European *Giotto* probe makes first close flyby of a comet (Halley's).

August 25, 1989 *Voyager 2* makes first flyby of Neptune.

April 24, 1990 Launch of Hubble Space Telescope.

July 4, 1997 *Mars Pathfinder* and *Sojourner* rover land on Mars.

November 20, 1998 First part of International Space Station launched.

2000 Humans permanently living in space on International Space Station.

SPACE OBJECTS AND ECLIPSES

COMETS

Most frequently seen
Comet Encke goes around the Sun
once every 3.3 years.

Most famous
Halley's Comet, which features in
the Bayeux Tapestry, was last near
Earth in 1986 and is due back in
about 2061.

METEORITES

The biggest meteorite ever found lies
in Namibia, southern Africa. Made
of iron, it measures 9 ft (2.75 m)
long, and may weigh about 60 tons.

Oldest meteorites
Known as carbonaceous chondrites,
the oldest meteorites are 4.55 billion
years old.

ASTEROIDS

Ceres, the largest known asteroid,
measures 578 miles (930 km) across.

METEORS

Here are some annual meteor
showers to look out for, with the
maximum number of meteors you're
likely to see in an hour.

SHOWERS	DATE	MAX. NO.
Quadrantids	Jan 3–4	50
Lyrids	April 22	10
Delta Aquarids	July 31	25
Perseids	Aug 12	50
Orionids	Oct 21	20
Taurids	Nov 8	10
Leonids	Nov 17	10
Geminids	Dec 14	50
Ursids	Dec 22	15

LUNAR ECLIPSES

Here are dates of total lunar eclipses,
and where to experience them.

May 16, 2003
S America, Antarctica
November 9, 2003
S America, Europe, W Africa
May 4, 2004
Africa, Middle East, India
October 28, 2004
N, S, and C America, W Africa,
W Europe
March 3, 2007
Africa, Europe, Middle East
August 28, 2007
N America, Pacific, E Australia
February 21, 2008
N America, S America, W Europe,
W Africa
December 21, 2010
N America, Pacific

SOLAR ECLIPSES

Here are dates of total solar eclipses,
and where to experience them.
Always wear eye protection when
viewing a solar eclipse, and never
look directly at the Sun – doing so
can permanently damage your eyes.

November 23, 2003
Indian Ocean, Antarctica
April 8, 2005
C America
March 29, 2006
C Asia, Africa
August 1, 2008
China, Russia, Greenland
July 22, 2009
Pacific Ocean, China, India
July 11, 2010
S America, Pacific Ocean

FINDING OUT MORE

There are plenty of places you can visit to learn more about space and have a good time. If you get really interested in astronomy, you may want to join an astronomical society.

PLACES TO VISIT
Kennedy Space Center, Florida
Find out about getting into space. If you're really lucky, you could make a reservation to observe a Shuttle launch!
www.ksc.org

National Air and Space Museum, Washington, D.C.
The history is all here, including the spacecraft that went to the Moon and plenty of Soviet space artifacts.
www.nasm.edu
To find your nearest science and space center, try this search tool:
www.tryscience.org/fieldtrips/fieldtrip_home.html
For a local planetarium, visit www.ips.planetarium.org/ips-worldwide.html

SOCIETIES AND PUBLICATIONS
Joining a society is a good way to learn more about space. You might get to use society telescopes and go on trips. Look for information at your local library, or at the Astronomical League (www.astroleague.org).

If you want to get a monthly sky chart, and keep up with what's going on, try the magazine *Astronomy*. More advanced is *Sky and Telescope*. Both magazines carry advice on buying telescopes and binoculars.
See *Astronomy* online at: www.astronomy.com

In Canada, visit the Royal Astronomical Society of Canada's Young Astronomers National Youth Group at www.rasc.ca/member/young.htm

USEFUL WEBSITES
www.nasa.gov
There are many sites of interest at NASA, the US space agency.
www.spaceflightnow.com
Keep up with all the latest space and astronomical discoveries and Shuttle launches.
www.seti.org
Find out about the search for life in the Universe at SETI, the Search for Extraterrestrial Intelligence.
www.heavens-above.com
Find out when to look for the International Space Station and other satellites from your backyard.
http://hubblesite.org
Look up the latest information about the Hubble Space Telescope.

SPACE GLOSSARY

Words in *italics* have their own entry.

Asteroid
A chunk of rock or metal in space.

Atmosphere
A layer of gas held around a *planet* by its *gravity*. Also the outer layers of a *star*.

Atom
The smallest part of an *element*, made up of subatomic particles – protons, neutrons, and electrons.

Axis
An imaginary line through the center of a *planet*, *moon*, or *star*, around which the object rotates.

Background radiation
A faint radio signal in space – the afterglow of energy from the *Big Bang*.

Big Bang
The violent event that created the *Universe* 12–13 billion years ago.

Black hole
A collapsed object with *gravity* so strong that nothing – not even light – can escape it.

Brown dwarf
An object smaller than a *star* but larger than a *planet*. It produces heat, but no light.

Comet
An orbiting lump of ice and rock that forms tails when warmed during its passage close to the Sun.

Constellation
A pattern of *stars* in an area of the night sky, often named after a character from mythology.

Dark matter
Invisible *matter* that is thought to make up much of the *mass* of the Universe.

Dust
Tiny particles left over from passing *comets* or from the formation of the *Solar System*.

Eclipse
An effect caused by one object casting a shadow on another.

Element
Any of the basic substances of nature, such as oxygen, hydrogen, or carbon, which cannot be broken down by chemical reactions.

Elliptical orbit
A noncircular *orbit*.

Escape velocity
The speed at which one object must travel to escape another's *gravity*.

Galaxy
A huge body of gas, *dust*, and billions of *stars*, held together in space by *gravity*.

Gas giant
A big *planet* made mostly of a deep, dense, gaseous *atmosphere*.

Giant star
A *star* that is many times the size of the Sun. Sun-like stars become red giants. Stars with more than 10 times the Sun's *mass* become supergiants.

Gravity
Force of attraction between any objects with *mass*, such as the pull between Earth and the Moon.

Light-year
An astronomic unit, based on the distance light travels in a year (about 5.9 trillion miles or 9.5 trillion km).

Mass
A measure of the amount of *matter* in

an object.

Matter

Anything that has *mass* and occupies space.

Nebula

A cloud of gas and *dust*.

Neutron star

A collapsed *star* made up mostly of neutrons (see *atom*).

Nuclear fusion

The combination of *nuclei* of *atoms* (at very high temperatures and pressures) to form heavier ones. The energy source of *stars*.

Nucleus (plural nuclei)

The central part of an *atom*, containing most of the atom's *mass*.

Orbit

The path of one object around another, more massive object in space. *Satellites*, *planets*, and *stars* are held in orbit by the pull of *gravity* of a more massive body.

Photosphere

A *star's* visible surface.

Planet

A spherical object made of rock or gas that orbits a *star* and reflects its light.

Planetary nebula

The shell of gas puffed off by a dying *star* before it becomes a *white dwarf*.

Pulsar

A spinning *neutron star* that sends out beams of *radiation*.

Quasar

A distant *galaxy* releasing enormous amounts of energy from a small central region.

Radiation

Energy in the form of electromagnetic radiation (a wave, of variable wavelength, traveling at the speed of light).

Red giant

An old *star* that used to be like the Sun, now near the end of its life.

Satellite

Any object, natural or artificial, held in *orbit* around another object by *gravity*. Satellites range from space telescopes to *galaxies*.

Solar System

Everything trapped by the Sun's *gravity*, from *planets* to *comets*. Other *stars* have solar systems of their own.

Solar wind

A stream of high-speed particles blowing away from the Sun.

Spiral galaxy

A *galaxy* with spiral arms emerging from a central hub.

Star

A hot, massive, and luminous (light-producing) ball of gas that makes energy by *nuclear fusion*.

Star cluster

A group of *stars* held together by the force of *gravity*.

Sunspot

A cool, dark spot on the Sun's surface, created by the Sun's magnetic field, that stops the normal circulation of gases.

Supernova

The enormous explosion of a *star*. A supernova happens when a supergiant star runs out of fuel, or when a *white dwarf* explodes. See also *giant star*.

Universe

Everything that exists, from this piece of paper to the most distant *galaxies* in space.

White dwarf

The collapsed core of a sunlike *star* that has stopped generating energy.

INDEX

CREDITS

Dorling Kindersley would like to thank: Chris Bernstein for the index.

Additional photography by: John Garrett, Dave King, Daniel Pyne, and Steve Stott.

Alex Barnett would like to thank: The editorial team, the Space Now team at the National Space Centre, Leicester, England, for checking facts, and Seth Shostak for assistance with aliens and writer's block.

Picture Credits

The publishers would like to thank the following for their kind permission to reproduce their photographs:
a = above; b = below; c = center;
l = left; r = right; t = top.

Anglo-Australian Observatory: ROE, David Malin 14cr, 15c, 61; David Malin 62tl, 64br; STScI/NASA 65t;
Luciano Corbella: 24, 26–27, 28, 29t;
Corbis: Richard Cummins 72l; Jeffrey L. Rotman 73;
European Space Agency: 4tr, 70; NASA SOHO LASCO 34–35c;
Genesis Space Photo Library: Orion Optics 84b;
Ronald Grant Archive: 29br; 74–75;
The Image Bank/Getty Images: 71r;
NASA: 5b, 6–7, 13, 13l, 27t, 32tl, 39b, 41b, 42–43c, 43b, 45tr, 45b, 46tl, 51, 64–65, 85, 86–87; Dr. R. Albrecht, ESA/ESO Space Telescope European Coordinating Facility 50tl, 50tr; CICLOPS/ University of Arizona 44–45c; Don Dixon/Finley Holiday Films 3, 22–23, 88–89; Jeff Hester and Paul Scowen (Arizona State University) 16bl; Raghvendra Sahai and John Trauger (JPL), The WFPC2 Science Team 20C; Space Telescope Science Institute 49cr; US Geological Survey 7tr, 36–37, 38–39t, 42tr, 50bl, 90–91;
Natural History Museum, London: 55b;
Popperfoto: Jayanta Shaw/Reuters 6b, 83b;
Science Photo Library: 8r, 10–11, 17t 18t, 19, 40t; Chris Butler 9bl, 58–59t; John Chumack 84tl; Tony Craddock 35br; Colin Cuthbert 68tl; Dale Darby 54c; David Ducros 25b, 48–49c; Dr. Fred Espenak 80–81; Jack Finch 33c; John Foster 56–57b; Mark Garlick 9tr; Tony and Daphne Hallas 55t; David A. Hardy 64t, 81br; Max-Planck-Institut für Extraterrestrische Physik 26tl; Mehau Kulyk 67, 92–93; NASA 1c, 31c, 46bl, 47, 51tl, 68–69c; David Parker 76–77; George Post 82–83; Detlev Van Ravensway 52b; Jerry Schad 60bl; Mount Stromlo and Siding Spring Observatories 62–63b; US Geological Survey 8l.

Book Jacket Credits
Science Photo Library:
Victor Habbick Visions

All other images © Dorling Kindersley. For further information see:
www.dkimages.com